MANAGING CITIES AT NIGHT

A Practitioner Guide to the Urban Governance of the Night-Time Economy

Michele Acuto, Andreina Seijas,
Jenny McArthur and Enora Robin

BRISTOL
UNIVERSITY
PRESS

First published in Great Britain in 2022 by

Bristol University Press
University of Bristol
1–9 Old Park Hill
Bristol
BS2 8BB
UK
t: +44 (0)117 954 5940
e: bup-info@bristol.ac.uk

Details of international sales and distribution partners are available at bristoluniversitypress.co.uk

British Library Cataloguing in Publication Data
A catalogue record for this book is available from the British Library

ISBN 978-1-5292-1827-5 hardcover
ISBN 978-1-5292-1828-2 pbk
ISBN 978-1-5292-1829-9 ePub
ISBN 978-1-5292-1830-5 ePdf

Cover design by Liam Roberts
Front cover image: Nakada

Contents

About the Authors   iv
Acknowledgements   vi

1   Into the Night   1
2   Who Governs the Night in Cities?   11
3   Placing Night-Time Governance: In or Out?   22
4   Night-Time Governance Trajectories: A Public–Private Affair?   42
5   Night-Time Governance Trajectories: The Importance of   62
     Scale and Politics
6   What Night-Time Agendas?   74
7   Whose Night is It?   85
8   The Night-Time and the Pandemic   96
9   Urban Governance after Dark: Eight Propositions   104

Further Reading   111
References   118
Index   131

About the Authors

Michele Acuto is Director of the Melbourne Centre for Cities, Professor in Urban Politics and Associate Dean (Research) in the Faculty of Architecture, Building and Planning at the University of Melbourne, Australia. He teaches night-time governance in the Studio N programme of the Melbourne School of Design, and is academic expert for the City of Melbourne's Night-Time Economy Advisory Committee. Michele was previously Professor of Diplomacy and Urban Theory at University College London and Stephen Barter Fellow of the Oxford Programme for the Future of Cities at the University of Oxford. Outside academia, Michele worked for the Institute of European Affairs in Dublin, the World Bank Group, the International Campaign to Ban Landmines (ICBL) and the European Commission's response to pandemic threats. Michele is the author of, among others, *How to Build a Global City* (2022, Cornell University Press), *Leading Cities* (2019, University College London Press) and *Global Cities, Governance and Diplomacy* (2013, Routledge).

Andreina Seijas is a Venezuelan researcher and the founder of Night Tank, an international consulting firm specialized in night-time governance and planning. Previously, she worked as Urban Development Consultant for the Housing and Urban Development Division at the Inter-American Development Bank in Washington DC and as Teaching Fellow and Research Fellow at the Harvard University Graduate School of Design while completing her doctoral studies. Her doctoral thesis provided a comparative analysis of night-time governance in three cities – Amsterdam, London and New York – and analysed the relevance of new forms of urban governance, such as 'night mayors', to facilitate conflict resolution at night. Andreina also worked as Policy Associate at Americas Society/Council of the Americas in New York City and was the Information Manager for the Mayor's Office of the Chacao municipality in Caracas, Venezuela. Andreina has a communications degree from Universidad Catolica Andres Bello, an MSc in Social Policy and Development from the London School of Economics, a Master in Public Administration and Non-Profit

Management from New York University, and a Doctor of Design degree from the Harvard Graduate School of Design. She is one of the editors of the *Global Nighttime Recovery Plan*, a collaborative guide that gathers innovative practices and solutions to manage night-time environments in the context of the COVID-19 crisis.

Jenny McArthur is Associate Professor in Urban Infrastructure and Public Policy in University College London's Department of Science, Technology, Engineering and Public Policy (STEaPP), UK. With an academic background in civil engineering and economics, Jenny completed a PhD in Engineering at University College London, focusing on urban infrastructure planning and policy. Jenny has broad experience in research and consultancy in projects based in New Zealand, the UK and the Gulf region. Before joining STEaPP, she worked as a researcher at the London School of Economics and Political Science's LSE Cities research centre for the Resource Urbanisms project. Prior to returning to university for her PhD, Jenny also worked as a consultant for local and national transport authorities and water utilities, advising on asset management and investment strategy. Jenny's research is focused on governance, planning and policy for urban infrastructure systems.

Enora Robin is a Leverhulme Early Career Research Fellow at the Urban Institute, University of Sheffield, UK. She joined the Urban Institute in June 2019 after having completed her doctoral research at University College London and having worked at LSE Cities. Her work focuses on infrastructure and social justice in cities, covering topics related to urban climate action, renewable energy transitions and transport provision. As part of her research, Enora worked with artist and film director Justyna Kabala and three nurses to produce a short film – 'Night Shifts' – narrating the experience of healthcare workers working across London hospitals at night.

Acknowledgements

As we stress throughout the book, night-time governance cannot but be a collaborative effort. In that, many have offered critical insights upon which this primer is built. We are first and foremost grateful to Pete Hawking-Sach, who provided much of the original research support, night-time expertise and impetus for the original study underpinning the book. A big thanks also to Anna Edwards and Shelby Bassett, who co-led Studio N and co-hosted the *Cities After Dark* podcast, for input into this project. In a similar vein, we would like to acknowledge Emilia Smeds' and Ellie Cosgrave's engagement in our night-time mobility and governance work in London, which foregrounds several critical sections of this book. Similarly, input into Studio N at the University of Melbourne by Simona Castricum, Jana Perkovic, Loren Adams, Will Gouthro and Clinton Moore has been important in shaping the direction of this work. A number of students who took part in successive versions of this studio have also been important in discussing the orientation of some of the case studies presented here, in particular, Thuy Anh Nguyen, Yewei Ni, Xinge Zhang, Kieran Boal, Alex McKenna, Suiyang Chen, Chengcheng Lai, Amanda Wiltshire, Wendy Cui, Sarah Moss and James Permezel. Input from the many researchers who took part in the *Cities After Dark* series is also reflected in several of the themes tackled here. Thanks, in particular, to Will Straw, Rob Shaw, Mirik Milan, J.C. MacQuarie, Alessio Kolioulis, Su-Jan Yeo, Ben Campkin, Lo Marshall, Michael Finchman, Theresa Jones, James Farrer, Chrystel Oloukoi, Roger Ekrich and Diana Raiselis. A thanks to Kate Murray and Bec Fary for support on that audio project is much needed of course. A special thanks to Tim Hunt at Arup too for the repeated engagement with our project and continuing support of our night-time adventures.

1

Into the Night

Introduction

Night-time has often been seen as the end of formal activities and the start of rest, respite or fun for many. Considered 'after hours', the dark period of our days has, in many contexts, been residual time for policy attention, public discussions and major initiatives beyond perhaps those emerging from the entertainment and hospitality sectors. Cities around the planet have been scantily planned for, imagined and debated at night. Yet, the night-time is all but inconsequential for our lives, especially on an increasingly urbanized Earth. All life on our planet experiences darkness to some extent. Most mammals are, after all, nocturnal. Around one in 15 employees in North America, and one in nine in Australia, work at night-time. Internationally, energy use tends to peak in the evening hours. Yet, precious little going on at night is still subject to scholarly and policy scrutiny. Here is where our primer for managing cities at night comes in. We take a cue from an emerging and, we would argue, exciting interdisciplinary crowd of 'night studies' (Gwiazdzinski et al, 2018), which has expanded over the last few years as a collaboration between night-time practitioners and scholars, and we step in with an intervention aimed at offering an accessible introduction as to why, and how, our cities' night-time should be governed. We start in this chapter by stressing this growing call of night studies to put the 'after hours' in the spotlight, and we make a case for both the importance of governing the night-time and the necessity to do so in a way that recognizes the value of the many international experiences out there, setting night-time governance as a trend, rather than a passing fad. We introduce here some of the grounding stances of this primer, as well as some of the core ideas emerging from the book and this mounting practice. For instance, we first meet: 'night mayors', as representatives standing in as voices for the urban night of many cities; the 'night-time economy' (often abbreviated as NTE), as the agglomerate of the economic activities (and people) keeping cities ticking after hours; and 'night councils' and other 'night-time governance' bodies, which have been designed in cities around the planet to formalize the way we engage strategically with what happens at night-time on our streets.

We should caution the reader that this is a world in fast evolution, not least because of the deep impact that the 2020 COVID-19 pandemic and its social distancing needs have had on night-time industries and activities. As such, *Managing Cities at Night* is but a snapshot in time when it comes to recounting the trends, directions and trajectories that night-time governance has been taking and will be taking throughout very diverse urban contexts that populate an increasingly urbanized planet. Our goal, then, is not to offer the definitive statement on this matter. Rather, our call is for scholars and practitioners to pay both closer and more systematic attention to what it means to be managing cities after dark, as well as one that is deeply steeped in both a social justice purpose that recognizes the many people underpinning these activities and an advocacy for a 'global' urban imagination (Parnell and Robinson, 2017) that can expand policymakers' and academics' world views. In doing so, we hope to encourage a new generation of urbanist thinking that does not 'clock off' at 6 pm but can rather thrive in the recognition that life, justice and opportunities continue, and oftentimes flourish, when the lights go down.

Putting the spotlight on night-time governance

The night has been taking a particular place in the way we think about cities in the 21st century. Many authorities governing cities, as well as community and private sector movements, seem to have been waking up to it throughout the last few decades. It has, in some places, become a focus of action and discussion as night-time themes emerge in policy and planning. Growing international attention to the NTE amid practitioners, as well as the potential of night studies (Straw, 2018) amid scholars, is now afoot. This is still the case as we write in the early months of 2021, even in spite of the lockdowns forced upon cities by the worldwide responses to the COVID-19 pandemic crisis. Evidence in support of this is now available across most continents and from many of the world's economic centres, but also from a widening cast of 'secondary' cities and towns. The media too has often been alert to, at the very least, some of these night-time issues – more now than perhaps at the end of the last century. Of course, this is still a form of attention that tends towards the opportunistic news story and the occasional but rarely systematic look into how cities are being managed after dark. London's launch of a '24-hour' subway ('night tube') service in the summer of 2016, for instance, raised interest across commentators in major international news outlets. In the same city, the tragic death of a woman kidnapped by a police officer while walking home at night in the winter of 2021 drove the resurgence of a wide debate on urban safety and gender issues after hours. The clash between local and state governments over the so-called 'lockout laws' for bar curfews in Sydney animated Australian media and policy debates repeatedly from 2014 to 2019. Paris's 2001 'Nuit Blanche' all-night affair has for quite some time – COVID-19 aside – been a common occurrence repeated in many countries around the world as a strategy to prompt after-hours tourism and cultural exchanges. The examples of night-time activity, in short, abound.

Across very different jurisdictions and urban development contexts, from the Antipodes to Latin America, East Asia and peri-urban France, steps towards formalizing the ways in which cities govern all of this have become increasingly common. Amsterdam's election of a 'night mayor' in 2003 as the official voice for the night-time has created, for instance, a mounting interest in the idea of cities having a representative for the NTE. Night 'managers' (like in Sydney), 'czars' (as in London) and other variations on this form of representative for the after hours have followed suit in cities as different as New York, Tbilisi, Madrid and Asunción. At the same time, numerous cities have been experimenting with alternative forms of night management or convening night-time conversations, as with Berlin's now much-chronicled 'Club Commission' and the many 'night councils' convening NTE interests and debates in cities like Nantes and Manchester. Therefore, we could argue with quite solid evidence that these are not just anecdotal vignettes to be relegated to minor news reports. Cities the world over are turning a closer eye to the night-time, and this has the potential to shape substantially the management of our neighbourhoods, streets and squares. This is a book about that potential, the ways it is being managed (or not) across the globe and the value of night-time thinking for urban governance. We would like to, so to speak, take urban policymakers into the night.

Managing Cities at Night aims to provide an accessible primer to the 'case for the night' in urban governance: why does the 'after hours' matter in cities? What, and who, is the NTE made of? Why has it been neglected, and why would it be an important domain for urban policy, planning and design going forward? What can we learn from the many examples of cities tackling this in both the Global North and South? How is night-time activity and its governance being called into question by the contemporary challenges brought about by the COVID-19 pandemic? Offering preliminary answers to these questions, the book's audience is twofold. First, it is aimed as both an introductory review for those that have not yet engaged with this theme and would like to know more. However, second, we hope it also stands to equip those working in the NTE and policymaking, whether they are within local government or elsewhere, with more evidence-based and scholarly propositions as to why their area of specialization is central to the future of cities. We seek to offer: a brief context of the emerging field of night-time governance and its mounting recognition; a short history of the NTE and some tangible classifications of the ways in which it is managed; and a review of what core challenges the night purports to pose for urban policymakers, private actors and scholars.

To step into the night, scholars and practitioners need, first and foremost, to understand that the night has become increasingly visible as an exclusive time-space and point of interest for policy and governance agendas in some cities around the world. This emergence of the night as an area of focus for city management and the provision of services has been encouraged by the aspirations of many cities to become a '24-hour city' and the discussions surrounding this economic, policy and discursive shift (Crary, 2013). This has led to the production of evidence and the creation of dedicated urban policy agendas relating to the promotion and marketing of cultural and creative urban spaces and regions (Landry, 2000), as well as consumption-led initiatives (Chatterton and Hollands, 2002; Hobbs et al, 2005; Roberts, 2006).

Earlier city-based policy and strategic initiatives regarding these nocturnal agendas have fallen thus far explicitly under the aegis of the NTE, with varying approaches and categorizations affiliated with the concept. This is especially true in Europe and North America, the voices of which have dominated night-time research for quite some time. Broadly speaking, as noted earlier, the NTE has mainly encompassed activities related to the entertainment and hospitality sectors. This means policy issues such as venue licensing (mainly for nightclubs and bars), hospitality regulation and matters pertaining to the support, management or externalities of leisure activities, as well as planning for cultural venues and night-time events in some cases. In some, generally less common, contexts, this is also taken to aspects of transport planning, street safety and compliance with public order issues, as well as, of course, the policing of the after hours. To date, early definitions and practices associated with the NTE, mainly emerging from North America and Europe, have contributed to many of the temporal frameworks attributed to the night in cities. This brings up an important definitional matter that, far from being just about semantics, is an essential backgrounder to what policymakers and scholars might mean when they speak of the (urban) 'night'. Definitions vary across many examples in this book, utilizing the end of the working day (5 pm/6 pm) as a key indicator in shifts towards evening and night-time activity in cities. Yet, this is by all means nowhere an established reality worldwide. Although darkness is often implicit in the imagination when considering the night, it is these temporal boundaries of, for example, 6 pm to 6 am in the case of London (GLA,

2018a) and Toronto (Toronto, 2018), and between 9 pm and 5 am in Sydney (Sydney, 2011), that are used to delineate the start and end of the NTE for many cities. Yet, cultural contexts also contribute to delineate this, with numerous realities in, for instance, the Middle East and South Asia ascribing different connotations to what happens 'after dark' in particular periods of the year (for example, Ramadan or regular night market traditions). Therefore, to date, while some of the most visible cities in terms of the NTE have adopted the '6 pm to 6 am' definition to refer to their NTE, the lack of a shared approach both complicates comparative analyses and opens up issues with the transferability of models from one city to another. From this point of view, we would both caution the reader against simply taking our primer as a shopping list of easily implementable policy solutions, and foreground our comparative effort as one representing a variation on a common theme (that of night-time management), rather than an illustration of a single dominant approach. As a 2015 study by British engineering firm Arup noted in respect to questions of design and lighting (Lam et al, 2015), we encourage the reader here to 'rethink the shades of night' in the direction of an approach that puts the emphasis on more context-sensitive considerations that focus on how people inhabit the night-time and its 'grey' spaces, rather than starting from the economic activities per se.

From that perspective, and still keeping a particular focus for our inquiry on matters of governance, we can point at a set of specific policy issues commonly emerging internationally. In particular, within the efforts to regulate, manage and govern the NTE, a number of related themes have arisen in recent years – which we tackle more in depth in a dedicated chapter of this book – going from licensing and operations, to night-time safety and liveability or the protection of vulnerable groups. Importantly, most cities across the world have begun to assess these issues through approaches in policymaking that involve partnership with non-governmental actors and strategic consultation with third parties. Across cities in Europe and North America, for instance, partnerships between representative groups from the alcohol and entertainment industries have seen the role of licensing, zoning and the protection of venues from closure become prominent issues for city officials when developing management strategies for the NTE (Roberts 2009). Some consulting and advisory services organizations have begun to focus on sharing best-practice examples concerning a wider remit of NTE management. Some have begun advocating for more holistic approaches to NTE businesses, safety and transport as key municipal agendas (Sound Diplomacy and Seijas, 2018). Of course, this is not just a story of advocacy and positive recognition. Rather, because of its specific focus on policy and politics, our international account is also rife with confrontations. For instance, in several cases, it has been the threat, or actuality, of music venue closures that has acted as a catalyst for discussion among stakeholders, residents and municipal officials (see Barrie, 2015; Harris, 2015). More broadly, these NTE clashes have been leading to campaigns and calls for consultation around best practice in managing the interests of the entertainment and leisure industries in relation to development, planning and residential needs. This is a central issue for our account of night-time governance, not only in an agenda-setting way, but also because in many of these highly political cases, cities have begun to formalize and institutionalize more tangible structures for governing the NTE. Such issues were prominent, for instance, in the formation of night-time commissions in Berlin and Zurich in 2001 and 2003, respectively, or in the appointment of London's 'night czar' in 2016. More generally, then, we would recognize that these discussions, agendas and confrontations have led the way in opening up further appraisals as to what constitutes the urban night, and which areas of governance must be addressed when planning and making provisions for this vast multitude of nocturnal activity.

Governing the night-time

The night is now being incorporated into urban governance in many, varied instances. Since the turn of the century, numerous cities – predominantly across Europe and North America but with growing purchase elsewhere – have appointed individuals and established offices with the task of managing their NTEs. Importantly, this movement towards night-time governance has predominantly taken place within urban and regional governance, with still virtually no *national* NTE policy available on the theme, in turn, stressing the importance of seeing this story from a 'city' perspective, as we suggest in this book. Yet, what is there to be governed, and how do we 'know' the NTE? Much of the early initiatives regarding this area of policymaking were generated from a strategic standpoint that promoted creative and cultural nocturnal exploits within cities as a means to foster economic growth through entertainment, leisure and consumption. The entertainment and leisure industries, centred on food, alcohol and, in some cases, tourism, were the primary focus of the NTE debate (Bianchini, 1995). In many cases, this went hand in hand with their perceived unwanted externalities, from crime to noise, light pollution and gentrification (Lovatt and O'Connor, 1995). The NTE was at the heart of scholarly discussion on questions of criminality and public order (Hobbs et al, 2003; Roberts, 2006), or economic development and downturn (Shaw 2010), throughout the 1990s and early 2000s. Since then, it has certainly gained purchase in several facets of both the humanities and social sciences, as well as the natural sciences, with concerns about animal behaviour and light pollution mounting in many different disciplines (for example, Hopkins et al, 2018). However, in recent years, dialogue on the NTE within academia and, in some cases, in policy has also begun to integrate the night-time requirements of urban dwellers and the challenges of how urban infrastructure attends to night industries' and residents' demands for inclusivity, equity, temporal availability and the management of after-hours services. Prolific strands of research have emerged on questions of night-time atmospheres and perceptions (Shaw, 2014; Brands et al, 2015; Edensor, 2015). Equally, particular vulnerabilities and questions of gender and race (Talbot, 2007; Nicholls, 2018), or space and society more generally (Mateo and Eldridge, 2018), are now well established in the study of how cities work at night. Engagement with night-time issues emanating from the progressive expansion of activities after dark, and, indeed, recognition of night-time life and livelihoods, has been thriving (Seijas and Gelders, 2021). Geographers (Shaw, 2018), political scientists (Acuto, 2019) and interdisciplinary groups of scholars (Kyba et al, 2020), among others, have even begun advocating for more institutionalized places for 'night studies' in the academy.

Yet, what does this mean for the governance of cities worldwide? How can this inform the ways in which all of this is practically managed by municipal, metropolitan and other forms of local government? How is the night, or 24-hour thinking, shaping the direction of urban governance? Who manages what happens after hours in cities in both the Global North and South? Until quite recently, when a sprawling and relatively diverse conversation on night-time issues started booming across continents, little was available to the municipal officer, private consultant or civil society activist when it came to discussing night-time *governance* more specifically (Straw, 2018). The 'policy mobility' sprawl of ideas and best practices to governing the night paved the way to this turn. Likewise, the emergence of a more exploratory and interdisciplinary night studies scholarship, usefully propelled by early-career scholars and research-practitioners (and, indeed, night mayors of various sorts), has laid a prolific ground upon which we can attempt to answer some of the questions outlined earlier in this book. Now more than ever, this is an important agenda, not just to economic growth, but also to recovery from the deep socio-economic impacts of the 2020 crisis ushered in by the COVID-19 pandemic. Here, we aim at picking this task up with an explicit goal to make this discourse and the variety of policy experiments in place around the world accessible to, and easily consulted by, a practitioner audience. This short volume offers an analysis of various governance approaches throughout numerous cities, seeking to provide a more explicit evidence base for discussions of the governance of night-time activities but without taking a particular sectoral stance or delving into more extensive scholarly debates (as we have done elsewhere).

The research underpinning this volume is a mix of a few separate strands of work converging into the main purpose of animating more informed, inclusive and internationalized night-time governance. The cases and evidence gathered here stem from original work conducted at University College London (UCL), the University of Melbourne, and Harvard University. They also emerge from debates taking place both in the aforementioned expanding academic debate around 'night studies', and through cross-border engagement between researchers, consultants and policymakers working in this field. Development of the empirical material presented here has involved, over the course of 2018 to 2020, through auditing and reviewing night-time governance structures, strategies and initiatives internationally. It has also included workshopping and diving deeper into some of these case studies, designed, in our view, as easily consultable snapshots aimed at night-time managers, as well as urban governance experts, practitioners and scholars more generally. Research for the book has also meant that we have drawn from our own experience of engaging in debates and discussions with students at UCL at the City Leadership Lab (now Urban Policy Lab) in the Department of Science, Technology, Engineering and Public Policy (STEaPP), as well as in the Melbourne School of Design's 'Studio N' course and research at the Connected Cities Lab (now the Melbourne Centre for Cities) at the University of Melbourne. Additionally, we have drawn from a study commissioned by the Inter-American Development Bank in 2018 to characterize the night-time activity in the World Heritage Site of Valparaiso, Chile. Given its history as a major merchant port and nightlife hub in South America, Valparaiso is undergoing a multi-agency technical cooperation to develop a new governance model to revitalize and enhance its Historic Quarter, with some nocturnal considerations in mind.

Desk-based and fieldwork research informing this book was originally undertaken from 2018 for the creation of a set of case studies as the basis of this volume, with a review of available strategic documentation and manifestos from city offices. This went along with secondary press releases and news reports, as well as (where available) academic literature. Key research aims were to chart the chronology of appointments of night-time offices, commissions, managers and mayors across the world, to analyse the structures of each governance model in respective cities; to map topics of discussion, pledges and initiatives, and to highlight any cross-cutting themes and policy implementations. As of December 2020, more than 50 cities were identified as having nocturnal-specific initiatives, strategic documentation and/or discussions concerning the management of their NTEs. A further 38 towns and cities in the Netherlands and Belgium (excluding Amsterdam) were identified through membership of the International Night Ambassadors Federation. These locations have not been included in the majority of analyses due to many of them holding night-time-related offices in a symbolic capacity, with night mayors and representatives largely elected in an informal role with little to no interaction with their respective city officials and departments.

In the interest of making the analysis of all these strands of work user-friendly for the city practitioner and the uninitiated researcher, the book uses various quick-reference writing styles, as with the provision of typologies or vignette case studies, seeking to illustrate of the modes of night-time governance available (at the time of writing) around the planet. In doing so, we hope our primer will serve not as an exhaustive breakdown of each city's approach to governance, but rather as a broad view of the genesis and progression of some of the possibilities for night-time governance that we have been witnessing across diverse cities. In that, we also present two chapters of more extended case studies that are not seeking to be complete guides to the likes of Tokyo or Sydney, but rather close glimpses into specific elements of what it means to manage the NTE. In our view, these are useful international examples that are often reported in simply anecdotal ways, and that can otherwise be read more systematically through the lens of urban governance that characterizes our narrative. The book highlights numerous shared themes and topics evident in night-time policymaking and discussion for the purpose of drawing some commonalities, without, however, seeking to argue that the NTE has been taking place equally across the planet. It also highlights the geographical concentration of cities in particular continents that appear to be at the forefront of these discussions, but in doing so, it makes an explicit (and we would argue normative) effort towards underscoring the need to decentre the Euro-American dominance that biases NTE discussions. From a policymaker perspective, we stress the relative infancy of night-specific policy, as testified to by the dominance of strategic vision documents, manifesto pledges and press-related materials over and above the availability of benchmarked outputs, as well as evaluations of existing policy implementations and extensive comparative reports. Our goal, then, is to open up even more explicit conversation on the governance of the night-time in cities, and to do so on the basis of an international and comparative look into the world of urban governance after hours. In doing so, we call on practitioners and scholars alike to think about these night-time issues in their broader global context, not just in their local specificities.

Overall, this book seeks to offer an exploration of the variety of night-time governance arrangements that exist in cities the world over, showing how and why different actors across the public and private sectors, and civil society, have taken an interest in the NTE. We then take a deep dive into the focus of night-time governance to discuss the type of night-time issues that have been particularly salient for night-time managers. We then discuss what has been obscured in current night-time policies, particularly issues of inequalities and the forms of precarity associated with night-time work. In exploring these issues of what has been called 'invisibilization', we argue that night-time strategies should be more inclusive and make more efforts to address the needs of night-time workers – this is likely to require multi-level partnerships with both governments and civil society groups within and beyond cities. Looking ahead and addressing the deep transformations that are likely to emerge in a post-COVID-19 context, we explore the impacts of the pandemic on NTEs and its implications for current and future night-time strategies. Our conclusion offers a series of recommendations for urban night-time governance moving forward. We hope that other urban researchers will take up this primer as a point of departure and redress these biases in favour of an even more proactive generation of researcher-practitioners striving towards explicit recognition of, and social justice advocacy for, the urban night.

2

Who Governs the Night in Cities?

Introduction

Whether we speak of night mayors, commissions or offices, and variations thereof, the current reforms towards night-time management have much to do with governance and urban policy. This is an area of direct relevance to a myriad of practitioners, as well as a political background to a vast variety of scholarly works, which we want to put an explicit emphasis on. Who governs the night in cities? This first research-based chapter of the book begins the investigation of how cities are managed at night through a comparative review of experiences from around the world, which stems from an explicitly political question regarding institutions and authority: how has the management of the 'after hours' of cities been formalized around the world? What we aim to do here is to kick off our 'primer' on night-time governance by looking at key lessons emerging from the recent movements to set up night 'mayors', 'managers', 'offices' and 'commissions' as tangible instantiations of night-time governance and comparing how these operate in diverse contexts. To do so, we offer some preliminary typologies of these night-time governance arrangements, framed mainly as both a graspable tool for practitioners to understand complex institutional set-ups in cities, and a guide for field researchers. When it comes to the age-old political science question of 'Who governs?' in the afterhours of most cities, and when it comes to the latest efforts by these cities as much as private sector and community groups to formalize an answer to this question, the evidence out there speaks of a thriving variety of possible responses and intriguing arrangements. In this chapter, we start from the individual roles that might be at play in night-time management, for example, mayors, 'czars' or managers, as well as the growing cast of nocturnal actors animating the ways in which cities are governed at night. We follow this up in Chapter 3 with a more institutional focus on the placing of these roles within or outside local government, and with a more direct review of what night 'councils' or 'committees' are.

A growing cast of nocturnal actors

Often referred to as 'man's first necessary evil', the night has always been subject to tight scrutiny and observation. From a spatial perspective, night-time activity, particularly larger nightlife establishments such as nightclubs, music venues and casinos, have traditionally been separated from other uses through zoning and alcohol regulations. However, the socio-economic impacts of these activities and the way they are distributed in urban areas have remained marginal issues for the planning profession (Roberts and Eldridge, 2008). For a long while, especially in the West but arguably also in many countries in the so-called Global South, the quintessential 'guardian' of the urban night has, of course, often been seen as the police, and not without criticism (Hadfield et al, 2009). While night-time policing was common, the cities and towns of early modern Europe did not employ any general daytime policing until the 19th century (Koslofsky, 2011). Today, most cities have dedicated police teams that monitor the streets at night, or overtime officers that work in conjunction with a vast network of surveillance equipment, such as ID scanners and CCTV systems. However, studies on the use of CCTV raise many questions on the effect of this technology over crime reduction and reveal that it only works in certain circumstances, such as closed locations (Welsh and Farrington, 2003; Norris et al, 2004).

Other actors, such as community and health services, the entertainment sector, or a wide populace of underground night movements, have also been proactive throughout modern history in 'managing' the urban night in very different and often poorly recognized ways. Yet, this reality has been fast expanding beyond a focus on either policing or public order, to a broader governance of the 'after hours' of cities that has been formalized and expanded around the world. Over the past three decades, the night has been gaining new prominence in urban agendas due to the positive contributions that the NTE has towards the revitalization and activation of city centres. While it has acquired a more positive significance, the night continues to be a highly regulated space where restrictive policies such as curfews and drinking bans are implemented to 'strike the right balance' between a flourishing and diverse NTE and growing residential populations (Jones, 2018).

Contemporary notions of urban governance refer to the process through which public and private resources are coordinated by a wide range of actors in the pursuit of collective interests (Pierre, 2011; Da Cruz et al, 2019). Similarly, urban systems of night-time governance operate at different levels and range from state actors, such as the police and community services, to non-state actors like business improvement districts (BIDs) and night-time advocacy organizations. In this chapter, we will describe the mechanisms and institutions involved in governing the urban night. While many of these mechanisms have emerged reactively and are on the fringes of the planning discipline, this chapter will also discuss the way in which the incorporation of new nocturnal actors such as 'night mayors' or 'night managers', as well as other night-time governance structures like night-time offices and commissions, have captured the interest of this field.

While local governments are still a central player, city planning involves a continuous process of negotiation, in which non-elected urban actors are attaining ever-growing significance in setting agendas, making policies and, indeed, implementing public services (Seijas and Gelders, 2021). Aside from city governments and the police, night-time management involves a diverse mix of agencies, including licensed venues, private security, residents and visitors to nightlife districts. These groups constitute new 'surveillant assemblages' in urban nightlife districts where different systems are brought together (Van Liempt, 2015).

Broadly, then, we could argue that four main types of 'nocturnal assemblage' are involved in managing the urban night (Seijas, 2020b):

- **Official trade organizations**, such as hospitality groups and bar and restaurant associations that represent a big sector of the local nightlife industry and lobby for its interests. Some trade associations are formal institutions that represent city or countrywide interest groups, such as local chambers of commerce, New York City's Hospitality Alliance or the UK's Night Time Industries Association (NTIA). Others are less formal or temporary arrangements to raise awareness of the needs and interests of night-time businesses.
- **Best-practice schemes and accreditations**, such as the Purple Flag and Best Bar None programmes in the UK. These government-backed schemes emerged as a response to rising media concerns about youth violence, inebriation and antisocial behaviour around the NTE. Their goal is to raise local quality standards and broaden the appeal of town and city centres at night.
- **Square guardians or brigades of volunteers**, created by cities and neighbourhoods to keep streets safe at night, particularly those with a high concentration of licensed venues. Examples include Les Pierrots de la Nuit (loosely 'night comedians'), an association of performers introduced in Paris in 2014 to prevent noise disturbances around nightlife activities, such as restaurants, bars, nightclubs, concert halls and festivals. Similar initiatives to experiment with 'softer ways of policing' night-time activity have been introduced by Dutch cities, such as Rotterdam and Amsterdam, in the

form of 'square hosts' or groups of civilians that monitor nightlife districts and help manage minor crimes and offences without involving the police.
- **Night councils and commissions**, which are independent or official bodies created to oversee nocturnal issues. Between 2001 and 2003, Berlin and Zurich established independent Club and Bar Commissions to represent the interests of the nightclubbing and bar communities, while San Francisco established an Entertainment Commission to manage and regulate nightlife and entertainment venues in the city. Many of these organizations are responsible for creating negotiated agreements, which are charters or documents that establish basic rules of coexistence in highly saturated nightlife areas, usually expressed in written form. Examples include the *Chartes de la vie nocturne* ('Nightlife charters') in French cities, the Safe Nightlife Covenants in the Netherlands and the Jungbusch agreement in Mannheim, Germany (Seijas, 2020b).

A recent addition to this growing cast of actors is the role of 'night mayors', individuals and teams responsible for governing nightlife and facilitating its harmonious coexistence with other uses, particularly in increasingly mixed and gentrified urban areas.

The 'night mayor'

Night mayors – also called 'managers' and 'czars', among other designations – are usually individuals selected by cities to act as a liaison between nightlife establishments, citizens and local governments. Variations of the 'night mayor' title include 'night-time economy manager', 'nocturnal delegate', 'nightlife advocate' and 'night ambassador' (Seijas and Gelders, 2021). The role of the night mayor was pioneered in the Netherlands. In the 1970s, the late Dutch poet Jules Deelder's prominent role in the cultural life of Rotterdam earned him the nickname of '*nachtburgemeester*' ('night mayor') of the city. Over the past ten years, Dutch cities have appointed more than 30 night mayors. The most notable of these representatives is the Amsterdam night mayor, a position elected for the first time in 2003, when the city formalized the Night Watch Conglomerate as an independent foundation to act as a facilitator between city hall and key stakeholders, and elected its first night mayor in the same year. From then up until 2012, the remit of the Amsterdam night mayor and their respective team was to promote key nocturnal events in the city, advocate for improved anti-discrimination measures and identify opportunities for safer, more inclusive night spaces in the city (Williams 2008).

The election of Mirik Milan as night mayor in 2012 brought about further change, as the Night Mayor's Office in Amsterdam, under Milan's leadership, successfully lobbied for the introduction of 24-hour licences in a number of venues across the city. Milan also introduced a pilot project of 'square hosts' in Rembrandtplein, one of the city's three main nightlife districts that comprises many bars, clubs and venues. The project involved hiring a group of volunteers to act as stewards at night, promoting 'soft enforcement' as a crime deterrent in public spaces. These initiatives can be seen as precursors to many other cities' approaches to managing 'the night'. In 2014, the night mayor role was institutionalized through the creation of Stichting N8BM A'DAM – an independent non-profit organization that provides guidance to the mayor and the city council on how to design policies to promote a culturally, socially and ethnically inclusive nightlife in the Dutch capital (Stichting Nachtburgemeester Amsterdam, 2018). Following Amsterdam's model, several night mayors, or 'night ambassadors', appeared in cities throughout the Netherlands. Although larger urban centres such as The Hague, Nijmegen and Groningen appear to have elected individuals that have a remit that involves lobbying city hall on behalf of the interests of citizens and proprietors concerning licensing and safety, night mayors largely occupy a symbolic role, without direct involvement in the shaping of policy in their towns or cities.

Prior to Amsterdam, between 2001 and 2003, Berlin, Zurich and San Francisco had made comparable efforts to establish offices or third-party organizations that dealt with nocturnal issues, and these were executed in the case of San Francisco (by proxy) through the Entertainment Commission at city hall, and in Berlin and Zurich through the establishment of independent Club and Bar Commissions that represented the interests of the nightclubbing and bar communities. The variety of night-time commissions set up by cities like Berlin, Zurich and San Francisco, and even Amsterdam's Night Watch Conglomerate, can be seen as precursors of the night mayor role, which gained greater prominence and media attention than its predecessors. A timeline of night mayors, commissions and night-time advocacy organizations can be found in Figure 1.

While night mayors' and commissions' responsibilities vary significantly from city to city, most of them have been created with a common goal in mind: mediation. However, their scope tends to evolve and diversify with time as they become empowered with new data and gain new access to city networks and resources. Their contributions can be categorized into five realms: advocacy, mediation, policy, capacity-building and infrastructure (Seijas, 2020b):

- **Advocacy:** for instance, the urban night has been of particular value to LGBTQI+ communities, which have been historically recognized for their contributions to the vibrancy and unique character of neighbourhoods

Figure 1: Timeline of night mayors, commissions and night-time advocacy organizations

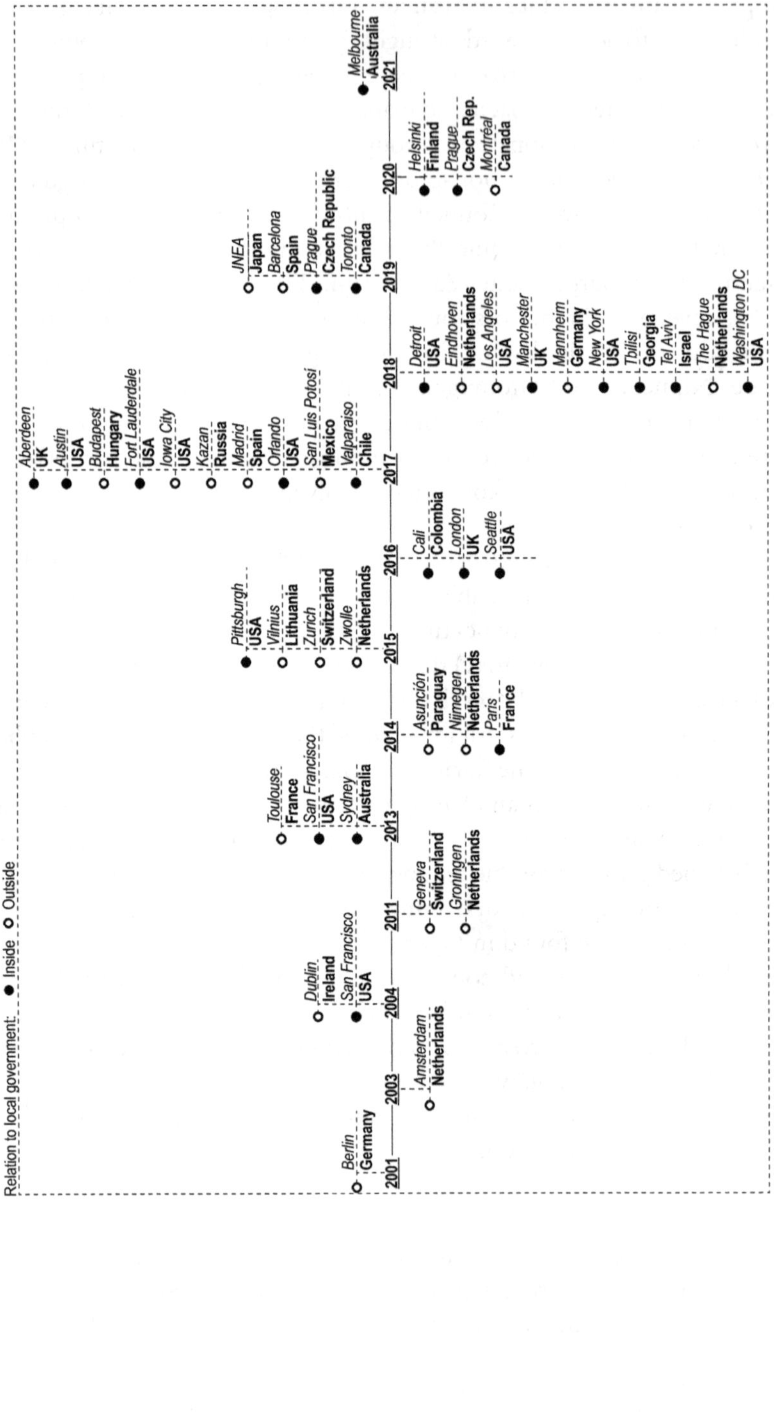

Source: A prior version of this figure was published in Seijas and Gelders (2021).

and entire cities. Night mayors have become key mouthpieces for the LGBTQI+ community, particularly in cities such as New York and London, where they led World Pride celebrations and awareness efforts in the summer of 2019 (Abadsidis, 2019; *Broadgate*, 2019).

- **Mediation:** an example of mediation can be found in Prague, a city struggling with the rise of 'stag do' or bachelor parties that cause many problems with noise at night. In 2019, the *noční starosta* ('night mayor') led an information campaign to keep people from drinking in the street in order to maintain the *noční klid* ('night-time quiet') after 10 pm (Willoughby, 2019).
- **Policy:** some night mayors and their offices are helping to update policies to prepare their cities for local growth, such as the appearance of residential developments in existing entertainment corridors. For instance, San Francisco introduced additional planning reviews and acoustic assessments for proposed developments close to music venues. Along with the Planning Department, San Francisco's Entertainment Commission has the authority to conduct these noise assessments and is invited to participate in the review process (Sound Diplomacy and Seijas, 2018; City and County of San Francisco, 2020).
- **Capacity-building:** several night mayors have embarked on efforts to enhance their city's preparedness for both recurring and more unexpected events. This is the case with Washington DC's Mayor's Office of Nightlife and Culture, which provides nightlife employees with tools and technology to handle recurring issues, such as sexual harassment, drug use and underage drinking in nightlife venues. These trainings aim to optimize police resources and encourage enforcement only as a last resort.
- **Infrastructure:** an example of night-time infrastructure is round-the-clock public transportation, as well as initiatives that reduce traffic congestion and promote the safety of both patrons and workers. In 2019, Orlando's NTE manager launched a pilot programme in collaboration with Uber and Lyft to create a weekend ride-hailing hub in the Wall Street Plaza, a highly saturated nightlife area where large crowds of patrons concentrate once venues close, looking for restrooms, transportation and something to eat (Greco, 2019).

By December 2019, almost 50 cities had incorporated the role of the 'night mayor' or had an active night-time advocacy organization. While some cities have incorporated these roles as permanent positions *within* local government, others have designated independent advocates or organizations *outside* city hall. A typology and specific examples of these roles will be described in Chapter 3. Yet, we can already stress how, aside from raising awareness of a new set of socio-economic and cultural issues, this new role has encouraged local governments to pursue a more collaborative and participatory approach towards managing health, safety and quality of life that challenges traditional views of the urban night, both in literature and popular culture. While cities differ greatly in their approaches towards night-time infrastructure and regulation, there seems to be growing consensus around the need for permanent night-time governance structures responsible for crafting these strategies and overseeing their implementation.

Networking night-time governance

The sprawl of night-time governance models and initiatives across different countries is no isolated occurrence. Rather, what is already apparent from the evidence outlined earlier is that there are underlying connections between these places pushing for the formalization of night-specific governance institutions and advocating for recognition of the after hours. Hence, while individual cases speak of localized urban innovation, much of what we have chronicled thus far in terms of the NTE has also been taking place and evolving within the context of an increasingly interconnected reality for urban governance. This is an important networking factor that we would like to begin highlighting in our primer, and that we reappraise throughout the rest of the book.

At work here is a vast landscape of 'policy mobility' (McCann and Ward, 2014) that is taking place nationally, as well as internationally, between peer cities. This is a networked driver of the night-time agenda sketched out earlier. It underlines how the 'night mayors' movement, for instance, has gone hand in hand with common events, advocacy and reciprocal engagements by many of the cases highlighted thus far. Night-time policies, as well as the underlying lobbying and advocacy that often brings them about, have been 'moving' from city to city through networks of private sector collaboration, research or city-to-city partnerships, thus contributing to the spread of the after-hours discourse. What is likely at play here is, to some significant degree, the influence of a more and more 'networked urban governance' effect (Davidson et al, 2020). This is a reality whereby the mobility of professional circuits, conferencing, virtual connections, city networks and, of course, more-than-local civil society and research linkages have all allowed for some of the ideas and models experimented with by the cities discussed here to travel across borders and to be experimented with by cities in often very different circumstances to the original ones (Acuto, 2013; Blanco, 2013). This is essential because the of growing clout of the more-than-local circuits of knowledge, ideas and capital that underpin much of urban governance today and are key elements driving how cities evolve in their management of the night-time (Robin and Acuto, 2018; Acuto

Figure 2: Global distribution of 'night mayors' and night-time advocacy organizations

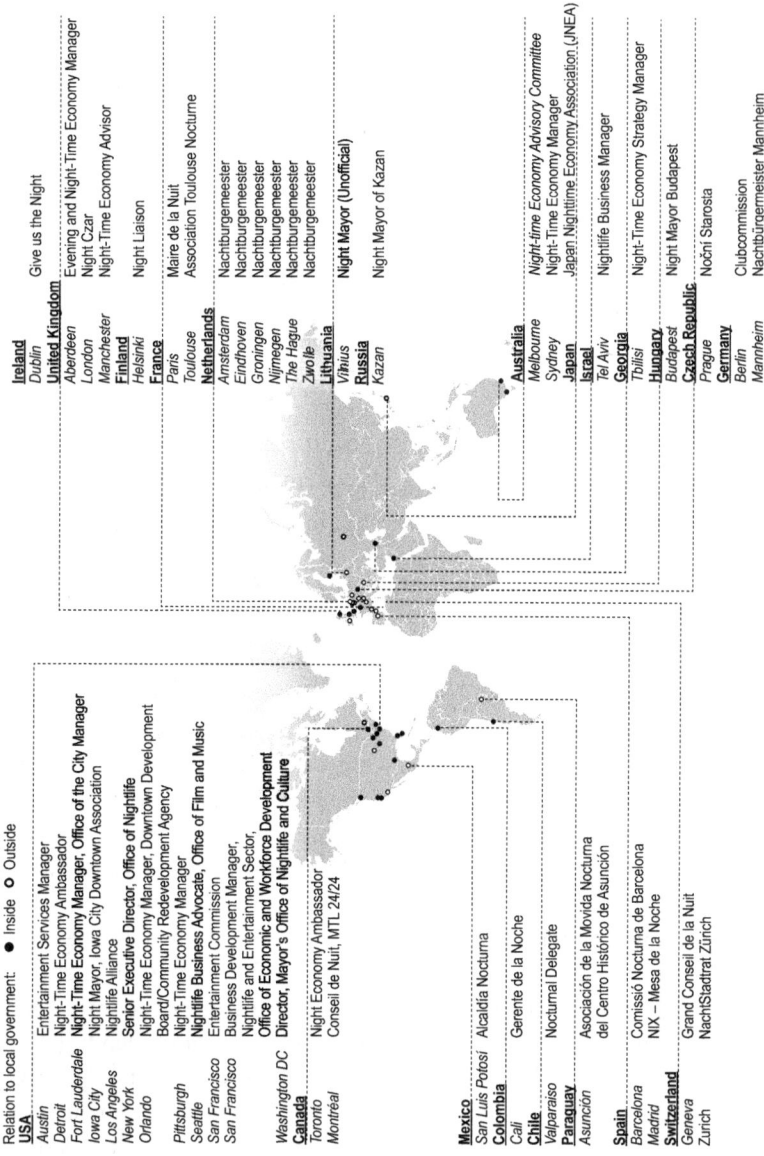

Relation to local government: ● Inside ○ Outside

USA
Austin	Entertainment Services Manager
Detroit	Night-Time Economy Ambassador
Fort Lauderdale	**Night-Time Economy Manager, Office of the City Manager**
Iowa City	Night Mayor, Iowa City Downtown Association
Los Angeles	Nightlife Alliance
New York	**Senior Executive Director, Office of Nightlife**
Orlando	Night-Time Economy Manager, Downtown Development Board/Community Redevelopment Agency
Pittsburgh	Night-Time Economy Manager
Seattle	**Nightlife Business Advocate, Office of Film and Music**
San Francisco	Entertainment Commission
San Francisco	Business Development Manager, Nightlife and Entertainment Sector, **Office of Economic and Workforce Development**
Washington DC	**Director, Mayor's Office of Nightlife and Culture**

Canada
Toronto	Night Economy Ambassador
Montréal	Conseil de Nuit, MTL 24/24

Mexico
San Luis Potosí	Alcaldía Nocturna

Colombia
Cali	Gerente de la Noche

Chile
Valparaíso	Nocturnal Delegate

Paraguay
Asunción	Asociación de la Movida Nocturna del Centro Histórico de Asunción

Spain
Barcelona	Comissió Nocturna de Barcelona
Madrid	NIX – Mesa de la Noche

Switzerland
Geneva	Grand Conseil de la Nuit
Zürich	NachtStadtrat Zürich

Ireland
Dublin	Give us the Night

United Kingdom
Aberdeen	Evening and Night-Time Economy Manager
London	Night Czar
Manchester	Night-Time Economy Advisor

Finland
Helsinki	Night Liaison

France
Paris	Maire de la Nuit
Toulouse	Association Toulouse Nocturne

Netherlands
Amsterdam	Nachtburgemeester
Eindhoven	Nachtburgemeester
Groningen	Nachtburgemeester
Nijmegen	Nachtburgemeester
The Hague	Nachtburgemeester
Zwolle	Nachtburgemeester

Lithuania
Vilnius	**Night Mayor (Unofficial)**

Russia
Kazan	Night Mayor of Kazan

Australia
Melbourne	*Night-time Economy Advisory Committee*
Sydney	Night-Time Economy Manager

Japan
	Japan Nighttime Economy Association (JNEA)

Israel
Tel Aviv	Nightlife Business Manager

Georgia
Tbilisi	Night-Time Economy Strategy Manager

Hungary
Budapest	Night Mayor Budapest

Czech Republic
Prague	Noční Starosta

Germany
Berlin	Clubcommission
Mannheim	Nachtbürgermeister Mannheim

Note: An interactive version is available at: www.nighttime.org/map

Source: A prior version of this map was published in Seijas and Gelders (2021).

and Leffel, 2020). In turn, the presence of these circuits sustains a growing populace of non-governmental actors advocating for greater night-time governance. Today, in practice, certain consultancies, such as the Vibe Lab in the Netherlands and Berlin, or Sound Diplomacy in the UK, as well as individual consultants and, indeed, academic experts (with an obvious reflexive meaning for us here), become important night-time governance actors and brokers.

Of course, the impact of policy mobility has already been the subject of not just wider geographical critiques (Peck, 2011), but also specific NTE-focused ones, for instance, questioning how the replication of external models further reinforces problematic neoliberal practices and strengthens the voices of those with economic clout at the expense of more marginalized communities (for example, Wolifson and Drozdzewski, 2017). Although we will dive into these challenges in more depth in Chapter seven, it is important to underscore this policy mobility base for the governance innovations depicted here because, as work, for instance, on Sydney and Geneva has illustrated, this means understanding how the state of localized governance at play in these cities is continuously subject to, or (more positively) in dialogue with, a changing political geography of broader connections (Pieroni, 2015).

This also underscores, as recent geographical literature has already stressed (Phelps and Miao, 2020), the continuing purchase of entrepreneurial forms of urban governance that have gone hand in hand with this networked approach to 'municipal statecraft' (Lauermann, 2018). Urban entrepreneurialism has characterized many of the night mayor experiments summarized thus far – whether they have been prompted by the private sector or by local governments. These entrepreneurial stances to managing cities, and thus their after hours, have widely backed the search for market-oriented and outgoing municipal policies, as well as the circulation of ideas, models and knowledge more generally about what could work in respect to, in our case, the NTE. There is, of course, a sizeable amount of literature that deals with these dimensions of urban governance, highlighting both possibilities and important problems that underpin some of their activities (Shaw, 2015). We have commented ourselves in several contexts on the caution needed when espousing these stances towards urban governance (Acuto, 2010; McArthur, 2019). From this perspective, without delving heavily and lengthily into a wide academic excursus, we should certainly stress the need for grounding even in a context of entrepreneurial and networked governance. Despite the variety of night-time governance set-ups that we have chronicled, engagement with communities is key for us here. For us, the plural 'communities', rather than the singular 'community', is a signifier of the expanse of which communities of night-time interest are at play in most cities, from business and night-oriented industries that have certainly been critical to the story painted here, to a complex of other community actors. Local interest groups, spatial justice advocates and bottom-up progressive initiatives have also left an important marker in driving greater attention to the night-time issues that we have already begun to highlight – calling for networking *within* the city and not just across borders and cities.

3

Placing Night-Time Governance: In or Out?

Introduction

Facts at hand, night-time governance seems to have been taking off in several cities around the planet, perhaps not as comprehensively as a truly 'global' movement, but certainly as a more and more visible international trend. Yet, where is the NTE governed? For us, the question of how night-time governance is 'placed' in respect to the organization of urban governance more generally is an essential one, especially for the many municipal practitioners and urban researchers focusing on this theme. Nuance, of course, would be required here so as not to simply pigeonhole styles of governance into easy categories. However, in this second empirical chapter, we suggest that it might be useful to start from a broad generalization: should the night-time be the purview of local government *within* the edifice of city policy, or should it be set *outside* of it? Of course, there is no easy answer to this query, but this simple differentiation helps us, we think, chart some commonplace realities within the multitude of examples we present here. Both realities emerge as equally productive and, at the same time, characterized by tensions, but in the meantime, they also help us clarify some initial challenges that night-time practitioners confront when trying to project a pragmatic stance on recognizing the value of night-time discussions in urban governance. In turn, as we illustrate, this also takes us to an additional type of night-time governance institution, that of the night 'council' (or 'committee' or 'commission'), which is perhaps as important in our story as the more widely chronicled and media-prone appointment of night mayors. We offer an initial typology of these institutions before beginning an initial foray into the common agendas that, whether within or outside local government, are emerging in night-time governance.

Where should the night-time be governed?

Who speaks for the night-time in cities? As we highlighted in Chapter 2, a growing aspect of night-time governance that has become a feature in discussions across many cities is the role of a dedicated representative for each respective city's night-time agenda. The position of the 'night mayor' has fast become well known. The popularity of the term has taken off particularly in the last ten years amid those working on NTE issues but is also increasingly in the public press. Despite the inclusion of the title 'mayor' in many cities' appointments, however, to date, the vast majority of these officials have had limited power in regard to policy amendment, policymaking and legislation. They have primarily been acting as representatives of, or to, city hall and mediating the interests of the industries that work within the NTE. Many of the individuals recently tasked with these roles have a background in nightclub and music event promotion and entertainment, and several focus on licensing in particular. In turn, this is reflected in much of the discussion concerning the kind of night-time governance that is being rolled out in local governments around the world. However, as we have already noted, it is also true that many of these individual representatives have begun to extend their remit and their dialogue to include a more holistic approach to the urban night and the provision of amenities and services. This means speaking of, and for, a broader night-time 'economy' than just the single sector within it that these individuals might hail from, be that the entertainment industry or elsewhere. In short, and as we will unpack more in Chapter 5 when looking at night-time agendas, the remit of urban governance 'after dark' is expanding, and the authorities entrusted with these activities are too. The shape and challenges of these authorities are the main focus of this chapter as we venture into the variety of institutional arrangements available out there beyond the case of the night mayors. If much attention has been paid by the media to chronicling and profiling some of this role, it is also important to recognize the multitude of other institutional set-ups that have characterized night-time governance across the world. As we outline here, the models and possibilities for managing what happens at night in cities are much wider than this specific role, and even in these positions, cities have differed substantially. We do so not to undermine the advancements brought about by these prime voices of the urban night, but rather to underscore the importance of context and variation, as against simplistic policy recipes, when it comes to institutionalizing a specific role for night-time thinking into the apparatus of local government (Straw, 2018).

Since the cases of Amsterdam, Berlin, Zurich and San Francisco paved the way at the outset of the 2000s, several other cities have adopted an open dialogue concerning their own governance of night-time issues.

At the time of writing, more than 50 cities around the world currently have a dedicated office related to nocturnal-specific issues. Many have an appointed or elected individual or body to represent key interests for citywide stakeholders regarding the night. While common traits can be found, and some typologies developed (as we do later), it is also important to stress the diversity of applications and the complexity of local conditions. Overall, and building on work we have already done to clarify how this international phenomenon has taken hold in cities around the planet (Seijas and Gelders 2021), we would argue that for clarity and practical applicability, the structures apparent in each city can be broken down into two main categories of classification, depending on their positioning *within* or *outside* local government. On the one hand, we have officially sanctioned night councils, commissions and offices, representing those realities situated inside local government and with a direct role in the formal govern*ment* of a city. On the other hand, we want to recognize those set-ups created as independent or 'arm's-length' offices or representatives, acting predominantly from outside the operations of local and metropolitan councils, representing a formalization of the govern*ance* of the night. Chapter 4 presents several examples of cities in each category, seeking to paint an international picture of how night-time governance is evolving. Two caveats are key here before diving into this analysis. First, night-time governance is fast changing around the world, not least because of the COVID-19 crisis. What we chronicle here are snapshots taken at the time of writing and by no means necessarily the very latest on that city's evolution. The goal here is not to have the most updated catalogue of examples but instead to paint a picture of the variety of ways in which cities can go about managing what happens after dark. Relatedly, we would then encourage practitioners to not simply pick and choose models to 'import' into their contexts, and scholars to dig deeper into the sociocultural realities that underpin these stories (Bennett, 2020). In doing so, we also advocate for a more global view for both policy and academia that is conversant in this widening landscape and appreciates the possibilities of such a widening movement.

The limits to many offices' powers regarding policymaking and legislation mean that dialogue with numerous city departments and key stakeholders in the NTE, along with dedicated third-party interest groups, is integral to many of the listed cities' approaches. Irrespective of the governance structure listed later, it is apparent that each form of office – with or without an appointed individual to lead discussion – requires the cooperation and collaborative approach of other organizations, both internal and external to city hall. From this, the role of many night-time offices around the world is primarily that of a facilitator or mediator, bringing together representatives from external organizations, local government and numerous municipal departments to partner in the creation of new initiatives and agendas that concentrate on the temporal elements of existing policy and strategy in the city. We start from within this edifice of local government, moving then on to the world of urban governance more broadly and the NTE institutions that have emerged outside various city halls.

Governing from *within*: official night councils, commissions and offices

The majority of cities that have actively sought to establish and promote new practices, planning and communications regarding their NTEs have done so by creating in-house night-time 'councils' and/or 'offices' for the nightlife. These bodies are generally created by city hall, after varying degrees of lobbying by NTE advocates, and include the appointment of an often-salaried individual tasked with coordinating and representing nocturnal initiatives, and facilitating debate and engagement. In addition, these offices and commissions often act as interfaces between public interest groups and industry stakeholders, sometimes with additional support by roundtables, interest groups and advisory boards, which generally include individuals and local experts with an interest in the local NTE. In several cases, the appointed individual in the role of night-time mayor/manager or commission/council chair is also tasked with acting as an 'on the ground' liaison between citizens/ proprietors and local government, listening to operational and residential concerns in situ, usually before collating responses and recommendations to members of the city council (or local government administration) in respective departments. In the following, we outline a sample of these initiatives in some of the cities we investigated, some of which we unpack more extensively as case studies in Chapter 4. The goal here is to sketch how the variety of institutionalization paths outlined earlier has taken place in several different urban political contexts, while starting with more tangible reference points on the world's 'atlas' of night-time governance. Without seeking to privilege any of these specific cases, we list them in alphabetical order in the following.

Fort Lauderdale, USA

In 2018, the city of Fort Lauderdale greenlighted a US$1.4 million budget proposal for a dedicated Night Time Economy Management Team at City Hall. The Night Time Economy Management Team comprises maintenance workers, a senior code compliance officer, a public safety aide, three police officers, one police sergeant, one fire inspector and one assistant to the city manager (Fort Lauderdale, 2018: 6). In 2018, the city also appointed its first NTE manager, Sarah Hannah-Spurlock, a previous city manager (for Key West, Florida), who will oversee the Night Time Economy Management Team's operations and liaise with residents and NTE stakeholders in the city.

London, UK

In 2016, then Mayor of London Boris Johnson established London's first Night Time Commission, an independent six-month advisory board inquiry to help realize the mayor's vision for London as a 24-hour city. The commission provided independent advice to the Greater London Authority regarding opportunities for the development of the city's NTE. Towards the end of 2016, Mayor of London Sadiq Khan appointed Amy Lamé as the city's night czar to act as a champion for the city's nightlife and to act as a liaison between London-wide citizens, stakeholders, businesses and city hall. In 2017, a network comprising one representative (though not always the same person) from each of London's 33 local authorities to act as night-time borough champions and to support the work of the night czar and the Night Time Commission was formed, also followed by a bespoke Late Night Transport Working Group. (This case is detailed in more depth in Chapter 4.)

Nantes, France

In 2013, Arnaud Tesson and Vincent Beillivaire were elected in an informal capacity as night mayors for Nantes. They campaigned for a night council to be instigated from city hall, a recommendation adopted by the city's mayor. In 2014, the Nantes Conseil de la Nuit ('Nantes Night Council') was introduced and Benjamin Mauduit, City Councillor for Nantes Metropole, was placed in charge of the council and its activities. Different from other cases, the council does not have a fixed composition of members and representatives; rather, the city explicitly encourages broad participation and open expressions of interest by citizens, associations and professionals interested in taking part in one of the *ateliers* of the council.

New York City, USA

In 2017, Council Member Rafael Espinal introduced a bill for New York to establish an office for nightlife, along with a dedicated executive director to oversee operations and relations between local businesses, communities and city government. In 2018, Ariel Palitz, a New Yorker with experience in the running of nightlife venues and community engagement, was appointed Senior Executive Director of the Office for Nightlife. The Office for Nightlife is based within New York City's existing Office for Media and Entertainment. It is supported by a Nightlife Advisory Board (an all-volunteer, 14-member, two-year-term independent body) making independent recommendations to the office, mayor and city council on issues affecting the nightlife industry. (This case is detailed in more depth in Chapter 4.)

Paris, France

Since 2014, the city of Paris has had a dedicated Paris Conseil de la Nuit ('Night Life Council'), led by the deputy mayor for night life and cultural economy. The Night Life Council consists of representatives from the city of Paris, prefecture of Paris, Île-de-France, Parisian police force, Tourism Office (regional and national) and various local associations. The council supports policymaking, regulation and other strategic activities for the night-time in Paris, and its approach is stressed in a specific 'Manifeste de la Vie nocturne' ('Manifesto for the Nightlife').

Rennes, France

In 2016, Rennes established its Nightlife Council, with commitment from the local government. Rennes had already authored a Nightlife Charter in 2009, which was revised and updated in 2015, adopted by the mayor of Rennes in 2016, and foregrounded the launch of the council. The council contains representatives from various municipal authorities, local residents and proprietors, the police, health and prevention workers, and prominent nightlife industry figures, and has been engaged with a revised charter, the *Charte Rennaise de la vie nocturne* ('Rennes' nightlife charter') reiterating and extending the commitments of 2009 (Rennes, 2016).

San Francisco, USA

In 2003, the city of San Francisco established an Entertainment Commission to manage and regulate nightlife and entertainment venues in the city. The commission's remit largely covers permit and licensing issues for citywide establishments. Responsibility for this work has since moved to the Office for Economic and Workforce Development (OEWD). Since 2014, Ben van Houten, as nightlife officer and then business development manager, Nightlife & Entertainment Sector within the OEWD, has acted as lead contact and coordinator for the San Francisco nightlife initiative Nightlife SF, with expansion into other policy areas now visible, such as late-night transport.

Sydney, Australia

Despite not having a specific nightlife office, the city of Sydney has a dedicated night-time city manager role and Night Time City project, which led to a dedicated night-time strategy ('Open Sydney') from 2013. In 2018, the city announced a 15-expert Nightlife and Creative Sector Advisory Panel to assist with continued efforts to manage the city's night-time and creative economies. Routinely, the city undertakes extensive research and public consultations regarding its NTE. (This case is detailed in more depth in Chapter 4.)

With a similar working remit to those cities that have created night-time departments and offices, there are a number of cities, such as those we list in the following, that have appointed individuals to work in a strategic management and coordination role regarding their NTEs. These individuals are tasked with coordinating existing offices and municipal departments that have a stake in the city's nocturnal operations in a sole capacity, and often focus on particular zones or areas of interest in their respective city, as is the case with Downtown Orlando, Iowa City and Aberdeen. As with the cases of night councils and commissions, in the following, we point to a set of examples of night-time mangers and associated roles in some of our study's cities.

Aberdeen, UK

In 2017, Aberdeen Inspired, the city's downtown BID team, appointed Nicola Johnston as Scotland's first night-time manager to promote the city's nightlife and broaden its appeal. The role spearheaded a further 'first' in Scottish urban governance with the launch in 2019 of the Aberdeen Night Time Commission, with a process of public consultation running through the last months of the year and just before the 2020 crisis began to hit the country. The commission has been working hand-in-hand with a larger cast of local governance, such as public transport businesses, community councils, universities and health sector actors, represented in the Aberdeen City Centre Partnership.

Cali, Colombia

Alejandro Vasquez Zawadsky, former President of Cali's Association of Nightlife Owners (ASONOD), was appointed as Cali's Gerente de la Noche ('nightlife manager') in 2016, becoming the first city in Latin America to create this role. Within that year, Cali held a 'Cali 24 hours' summit, inviting Mirik Milan, then Night Mayor of Amsterdam, to share experience and knowledge around planning for the NTE. Despite its initial institutional boost and great support from local and national media, the position was later relocated under the Tourism Department following a major process of restructuring within the municipality. This move diluted its initial focus and resources geared at diversifying the city's night-time activity, and paved the way for the disappearance of the role in 2017.

Iowa City, USA

Iowa City is currently the only city that has mandated night-time working hours for its night-time manager/mayor. Starting in 2017, Angela Winnike was the Downtown Iowa City Night Mayor, working primarily within the realms of culture-led promotion and safety. Her work as a liaison between residents and the city involved undertaking outreach, observation and engagement activities between the hours of 7 pm and 2 am from Thursday until Sunday each week.

Manchester, UK

Since 2017, the NTIA, an independent organization consisting of bar, club and restaurant owners from across the UK, has engaged with numerous cities regarding their current legislation, policing and planning for their respective NTEs. A prominent board member of the NTIA, nightclub and event manager Sacha Lord, spearheaded the creation of an informal Night Time Commission in the city. With the election of a new mayor of Greater Manchester, this resulted in the appointment of Lord as the city's new NTE advisor in April 2018, supported by a Night Time Economy Panel that will comprise experts from across Greater Manchester, leading to the launch by the mayor and advisor of a 2020 Greater Manchester Night Time Economy Blueprint.

Orlando (Downtown), USA

In 2016, a city-led Downtown Nightclub Taskforce Report assessed Downtown Orlando's needs for safer and more vibrant public space in the city centre, and recommendations were made for the appointment of a NTE project manager within the Downtown Development Board. In 2017, Dominique Greco Ryan, who has a background in hospitality management in the city, was appointed NTE project manager for Downtown Orlando and facilitates communication between businesses and local government.

Pittsburgh, USA

In 2015, Pittsburgh appointed Allison Harnden as the city's NTE coordinator. As ex-Vice President of the Responsible Hospitality Institute, Harnden has previous experience in advising cities on aspects of their NTEs through the institute's 'Sociable City' framework, which details approaches to night-time mobility, safety and partnership working, and the management of public space.

Tbilisi, Georgia

In March 2018, the Tbilisi Night Economy project was created to develop a strategy and action plan to promote the city's growing club culture and music scene. This involved setting up a team led by a night-time economy manager, who acted as a special advisor to the mayor in matters related to creating a more favourable regulatory environment for these activities to flourish, while handling issues around noise pollution and drug use. The project involved several initiatives, such as a night bus pilot project and the country's first International Night-Time Economy Forum, organized in 2019.

Valparaiso, Chile

In May 2017, inspired by the role created by Amsterdam and other European cities, Mayor Jorge Sharp designated a Delegado Nocturno ('nocturnal delegate'), who was responsible for promoting collaboration among residents and the nightlife industry, and reactivating the city's night scene in a safe and productive way. The person selected for the role was a former businessman and club owner, Juan Carlos Gonzalez. A study conducted between 2018 and 2019 revealed that rather than seen as an advocate or champion of citywide concerns for its night scene, the nocturnal delegate was perceived as a 'lobbyist' or promoter of the interests of the nightlife industry. Several council members and representatives of local groups criticized the lack of transparency of his administration and the absence of a 'master plan' with clear goals and expected results. Following corruption charges and allegations that he was 'leasing' liquor licences, the nocturnal delegate resigned in November 2018 and Mayor Jorge Sharp announced the creation of a Citizen Safety Division to help the municipality 'to better handle the issues in Valparaiso's night scene' (Seijas, 2020a). (This case is detailed in more depth in Chapter 4.)

Governing from *outside*: independent commissions, councils and offices

The majority of the cities listed in the following are prominent fixtures in global discussions around night-time governance, with Zurich, Berlin and Amsterdam, in particular, cited as pioneering cities in this regard. Each of these cities listed has its NTE thinking mobilized and facilitated by independent bodies, separate from city hall, which act on behalf of stakeholders and interest groups while lobbying and making planning and policy recommendations to city hall. What follows is a sample of these independent approaches.

Amsterdam, Netherlands

Amsterdam is often cited as the innovator in terms of night-time governance, as well as being named the first city to appoint a night mayor. The city first began discussions around night-time governance in 2003, with the appointment of a Night Watch Conglomerate, led by subsequent nightlife experts from the city up until 2012. The aims of the conglomerate were set out by local government officials seeking more constructive communication with nightlife officials. In 2014, the Amsterdam Night Mayor Office was established as a non-profit organization that is independent from the city of Amsterdam but works closely with local government in reconciling issues around planning and licensing, and with nightlife business owners (Amsterdam, 2018). In the same year, Mirik Milan was appointed Amsterdam's first official night mayor. Milan was replaced by Shamiro Van Der Geld, who was voted night mayor in 2018 at a public event. Van der Geld stepped down from his role as night mayor and chair of the Night Mayor Foundation in June 2019, less than 18 months into the two-year job. Official reports on the reasons for this termination refer to escalating tensions between him and his team, and the fact that he was dealing with too many tasks at once (Hawthorn, 2020). In 2018, Amsterdam's Night Mayor Office – similar to city departments of Paris and London – established a Nachtraad ('Night Council'), consisting of local experts and industry stakeholders, to help advise the Night Mayor Foundation's Board (Amsterdam, 2018b).

Asunción, Paraguay

In 2013, as part of a strategy and plan to reactivate the deteriorated Historic Centre of Asunción (CHA), the National Secretariat of Culture and the municipality of Asunción convened a series of meetings with restaurant, nightlife and entertainment businesses to analyse the role of the NTE in the CHA's revitalization. As a result of these talks, several restaurant, bar and club owners decided to create the Asociación de la Movida del Centro Histórico de Asunción (Association for Nightlife in the Historic Centre of Asunción [AMCHA]). Since its creation in August 2014, this association has organized more than 30 large-scale events that combined themes related to entertainment, art and Paraguayan history. AMCHA has also established partnerships with hotels, non-governmental organizations (NGOs), companies and public institutions linked to the tourism and cultural sectors. Through these activities, the CHA has become a new epicentre for entertainment, particularly among millennials and young professionals. Additionally, AMCHA's work paved the way for ongoing discussions on the creation of a specialized office that manages the area's night-time activity.

Berlin, Germany

Berlin has had a Club Commission in operation since 2001. The commission began by acting as a representative body for the city's nightclubs and its community of patrons. Over the past two decades, the commission has become increasingly involved as a requisite voice in planning discussions and advocacy work across the city, representing numerous working groups. The Club Commission has been directed by Lutz Leichsenring since 2009. (This case is detailed in more depth in Chapter 4.)

Geneva, Switzerland

The Grand Council of the Night has operated in Geneva since 2011. It actively promotes nightlife culture in the city and has a set of goals that underline its approach to its advocacy and engagement work with the city of Geneva, members of the public and nightlife business and stakeholders. It has an open membership policy, with the benefits of membership and opportunities for engagement chiefly rooted in the bar and nightclub industry in the city (Geneva, 2018). The council is currently co-chaired by Raphael Pieroni and Matthias Solenthaler.

Montreal, Canada

In the spring of 2020, MTL 24/24 – a civic organization formed in 2017 to push Montreal towards the development of policies for governing the night – launched a Conseil de Nuit ('Night Council'), an independent body that brings together 12 representatives from different sectors of night-time culture. Over the course of 2020–21, the council launched four committees regarding: health, security, diversity and inclusion; nocturnal lifestyle; clubs, cultural bars and venues; and festivals and events. Each of these developed proposals for the strengthening of Montreal's night-time cultural activity. MTL 24/24 defines itself as a civic organization open to all those with an interest in the night, rather than a professional body or lobby speaking solely on behalf of night-time venues or businesses. While typically acting independently of city government, MTL 24/24 has sought and been granted a voice in the elaboration of night-time policy. In particular, it has consulted on both an official and unofficial basis with Montreal's Commissioner of Noise and Night, who was named in 2020 as the first public official responsible for night-time policies in Montreal.

San Luis Potosí, Mexico

In 2017, San Luis Potosí created the civil society organization Alcaldía Nocturna to promote safe nightlife in this central Mexican city. Inspired by Amsterdam's model after participating in the city's Night Mayor Forum in 2016, Adelina Lobo created this independent organization to act as a mediator between city hall and nightlife businesses in her hometown. In 2017, Alcaldía Nocturna organized a Key of the Night music festival to raise awareness of the positive contributions that nightlife brings to the city, as well as the need to update local alcohol licensing regulations to enable a safer and more vibrant night scene.

Toulouse, France

Since 2014, Toulouse Nocturne has acted as a night council in the city. Christophe Vidal was installed as 'Mayor of Toulouse Nocturne' and has held the post since the organization's inception. Interestingly, the organization has taken an explicit focus on the 'right to the city' in several of its activities, including on issues of mobility and nocturnal accessibility.

Zurich, Switzerland

Since 2001, Zurich has had a Nightlife Roundtable, consisting of business owners, the police, local authorities and nightclub owners coming together to discuss topics of importance to the city's NTE. In 2011, the Bar and Club Commission was formed in Zurich by proprietors of bars and clubs as a vehicle to lobby and represent their interests publicly. There is now a membership base of 120 in the commission. Following the creation of the commission, an independent Nightlife Council was formed in 2015. This is an association without legislative power that aims to work with the roundtable and commission in representing the needs of patrons and nightlife users. All members within the council work on a voluntary basis. The Nightlife Council has no designated head, but Alexander Buechli of the Bar and Club Commission acts as a representative on behalf of the commission and is an independent consultant.

Not just mayors: what do night 'councils' do?

An important reality that emerges from the bird's-eye view sketched out earlier, then, is that of the multitude of NTE committees and night councils established in cities around the planet. These highlight how, while critical in many instances, night mayors and managers need to be seen side by side with often less chronicled types of NTE institutions. These are entities typically designed to gather input and advice, to represent night-time industries, or to review the state of the NTE in a particular city. They come in many shapes and with many names: 'night councils', 'committees', 'commissions', 'advisory boards' and more. These are important pieces of the night-time governance puzzle because roles such as those of night managers, or specific nightlife offices within local government, have also gone hand in hand with a multitude of consultation and engagement mechanisms that should not be underplayed. For our introductory purposes, then, it is certainly worth summarizing this variety of consultative and collective mechanisms here before moving into more specifically thematic discussions. Overall, we would argue that we can summarize the variety of committee-like institutional set-ups other than 'night mayors' and managers (as presented in the vignettes earlier) into potentially four categories detailed in the following to once again stress the potential of night-time governance and its burgeoning variety against one-size-fits-all approaches. These are four diverse ways of interpreting collective consultation on the night-time. Yet, of course, these 'types' can appear in a mixed fashion in several cases. They are, in summary:

- **Commissions**, whose role is to be specific-purpose bodies for reviewing and reporting on the NTE in cities, often for the specific goal of feeding findings into governance. They can be held ad hoc or in a continuing approach, and they tend to result in the formulation of strategic initiatives and reforms (for example, in London and New York).
- **Councils**, whose role is predominantly as broad industry and citizenry engagement bodies feeding NTE voices into local government. They

tend to operate through ongoing broad membership 'boards' representing the voice of the NTE in cities (for example, in Paris and Amsterdam).

- **Boards**, whose role is mainly to act as 'peak' NTE representative structures, typically emerging from outside the administration of local authorities and as non-governmental initiatives, which are often characterized by large and, to a degree, open membership (for example, in Berlin and Geneva).
- **Panels**, whose key role is to be a source of evidence and information for local governance authorities, including night mayors, managers and advisers, to draw on and engage with regularly (for example, in Sydney and Greater Manchester).

These are, of course, but ideal types, and in several cases, these approaches occur in mixed forms that conjugate two or three of these roles to some degree. This is the case, for instance, of Aberdeen, which mixes a council and expert panel approach to some degree, or Rennes, which mixes committee and council models. From this point of view, the typology just outlined is mainly a way to stress the possibilities of consultation and collective engagement when it comes to the NTE, as well as the value in institutionalizing these, while recognizing that this happens in many different shapes in cities around the world.

While the landscape of night councils and commissions is wide and certainly not just limited to the aforementioned examples, a few initial common traits have already emerged as important for consideration by practitioners when considering these collective governance bodies as a possible solution for their local concerns. In particular, we would identify seven main functions that night-time committees, commission and councils play in night-time governance, in no specific pecking order:

- providing strategic governance and policy advice, for instance, formulating key reports or conducting (expert and/or independent) inquiries into the NTE;
- representing the voice of NTE businesses, communities and/or citizens, and convening the city's conversation on nightlife;
- offering expert insight, data and specialist evidence as advice or complement to municipal policymaking on the NTE;
- highlighting a dedicated urban area or theme of particular value for night-time policymaking and governance, thereby putting a spotlight on the likes of key precincts, governance challenges or socio-economic areas needing specific or urgent attention;
- acting as bridge between the internal night management of a city (for example, by a deputy mayor, night manager, adviser, office or mayor)

and the concerns and views of external businesses, communities and/
or citizens;

• acting as general NTE management institutions to tackle major nightlife
  issues beyond the more technical remit of local administrations; and

• incubating and setting up more specialist taskforces and working groups
  targeting more specific areas of NTE governance, either via subcommittees
  or as separate bodies.

Importantly, it is worth underlining how many of these models and
experiences have been more or less formally connected with each other.
As highlighted in Chapter 2, this has often been the case because of the
inter-referencing and 'policy mobility' between cities in the setting up of
these models. This is the networked dimension of night-time governance
that we referred to in Chapter 2. Typically, more recent cases have often
been based on (and some in explicit dialogue with) prior experiences, as in
the examples of Manchester, Aberdeen or Paris. Many of the committee/
council chairs and night mayors/managers involved in these programmes
have been actively in communication and exchange with others, taking
part in forums and summits like Sydney's Global Cities After Dark or
London's recent NITE (Night Spaces: Migration, Culture and Integration
in Europe) Conference at University College London. Yet, it also takes the
shape of informal networks of practitioners and researchers, such as those
underpinning the recent development of the Global Night Time Recovery
Plan. The key issue here, then, is that of the value of seeing these case
studies not just as separate occurrences, but as part of a growing and often
internationally networked community of practice that can be tapped into
for exchange and insights – as our primer hopefully provides evidence of.

No one model, but common agendas?

We are not at the point here to throw a sweeping generalization about some
of the stories and lessons discussed in this book thus far. Yet, at the same
time, we want to begin to paint what appears to us as an important picture
of the variety of models of urban night-time governance – many now at
least a decade old.

The first critical issue emerging from this brief bird's-eye view of examples
worth highlighting is that of the 'depth' of governance of the night that
we can witness when we cast a broad international view on this issue. As
we have noted, whether by looking within or outside the edifice of local
government, the location and the placing of what can be considered as the
policymaking heart of how things operate at night-time in cities clearly

happens at a multitude of scales and through a multitude of public–private arrangements. There is, in short, a deep geography of urban governance in and around the NTE. Moreover, this takes place through a sizeable mix of contextual realities created by specific social and cultural conjectures, the political economies of which should not, perhaps, be easily flattened to our initial straw-man typology of 'in and out'. We should keep in mind that night-time governance happens very tangibly in relation to the broader realm of urban politics. This is a sphere that urban scholars and local government policymakers are certainly well versed in; however, it is also one that needs to be repeatedly highlighted so as not to forget that the way in which the NTE has been tackled also relates to broader regional and national economies. *NTE issues are inherently political issues*, even if they are not, at times, politicized. They deal with matters of powers, interests and political relations that, at times, might be forgotten when reporting specific stories or importing attractive models. For us, this means not to forget the way that night-time governance structures, whether formally or informally, take at least a cue from wider urban governance drivers, as well as bottom-up, community and business urban political initiatives. We would strongly advocate not to divorce the night-time from the bigger picture of the governance of cities, but rather, as we stress repeatedly throughout the book, to bring it closer to the centre of city politics, whether at the national, regional, metropolitan, local or even neighbourhood level – or a mix of these layers of government.

Nonetheless, we still find particularly useful the exercise of thinking about whether the governance of the urban night happens within the realm of government or in a wider sphere of governance. It is clear from the short excursus into the international cases discussed earlier that this differentiation already allows us to draw some common typologies and themes. This, in turn, can inspire a more structured and scholarly dialogue than that which might often be reported locally when looking internationally at models that could be emulated. We encourage policymakers and other night-time advocates to take it into account as an important measure of judgements for practitioners to understand the placing of night-time governance issues in the politics of the city. We have used it here to open up the discussion for the following chapters. This, conversely, highlights a number of key issues requiring deeper attention. So, what can we begin to say for certain about the possibilities and the challenges of managing cities at night here?

Overall, considering the visibility and traction of these cases, one could argue that many of those that started outside local government, as with Amsterdam or Berlin, originally gained much of the initial present-day attention and media traction. They tend to be common 'urban antecedents' (Bunnell, 2015) in the geography of inter-referencing of NTE urban governance models. They are recurring tropes and easily searchable case studies when it comes to speaking of the NTE and night-time governance in the way we currently do across continents. This is perhaps because of the role played, as briefly illustrated earlier, by their night mayors and their night-time commissions, which have congealed the discussion as to what the night-time means and could be leveraged for in many cities. It is also because of the global visibility typically afforded to these 'global' cities and the relatively wide circulation of information about their evolution reported in major globally present news outlets. Yet, as we will see in Chapter 4, this relatively recent account of night-time governance should not be blind, or short-sighted, to longer-standing histories of night politics that underpin many of these places. As we suggest doing in our comparative case studies in Chapter 4, we need to grasp these stories through a wider view of the historical trajectory of night-time governance in many of these places, and allow perhaps an even wider sense of what accounts for 'within and outside' local government. Further, it is clear that several of the prominent examples of the governance of the night-time emerging from within the edifice of municipal and metropolitan politics have also emerged to the fore as much reported on, such as in the cases of London and New York. The field of night-time governance, then, seems pretty wide open at present.

Certainly, it appears quite clear across most cases that the so-called 'core NTE', focused on entertainment and hospitality, is still very much dominant in the governance of cities after dark. In some cases, a slightly wider interpretation of this 'core' expands to the likes of transport or core services (for example, food and sundries). Rarely does it emerge as a 'wider NTE', accounting for busy sectors of the economy, or more broadly of society, which are deeply nocturnal, employ hundreds of thousands of night-shift workers and yet rarely make it atop headlines and policy foci. These are night-time employees such as healthcare and nursing workers, maintenance and environmental services operators, community services personnel, and many others. This is a 'core–wide' differentiation that has already been articulated effectively in considerations of the Australian NTE by our colleague Anna Edwards and consultants Ingenium Research in 2016–17 and again very recently in 2020 to characterize how policymakers have typically centred their attention on the core rather than the wider landscape of economic activities underpinning urban governance at dark (Ingenium Research, 2018). As we make evident throughout our primer, the potential for night-time governance to grasp, manage and engage the 'wider' NTE and the production side of it all, whether within or outside the 'core', is substantial.

From the perspective of what is already there in terms of key NTE issues tackled in cities, some key agendas stand out from the initial considerations about the institutions that animate night-time governance that we have chronicled thus far. We dedicate a whole chapter (Chapter 6) to these further on in the book, but a quick excursus is perhaps already useful here to set up Chapter 4's comparative case studies. Economic growth and vitality, as well as regeneration, tend to appear as a common trait across most of the cases depicted in this chapter. These mainly relate to issues of entertainment in some areas, as well as the arts and cultural industries, tourism, safety and, in some cases, transport in other contexts. Many agendas have to do with matters of land use, urban development and, of course, licensing of night-time businesses and operations.

Yet, perhaps what is 'not there' is equally interesting. This, we think, might be especially true if we aim to detail a more normatively oriented approach for night-time advocates, researchers and policymakers in order to drive a clear appreciation of night-time governance. Governance issues that relate to the sustainability of the urban night are scant. In many cases, the same goes for questions of well-being and health, especially before the pandemic hit. Similarly, the status and contribution of night-shift workers, the problems of night-time inequalities, and the question of the 'right to the city' at night (Yeo, 2020), which we again tackle in Chapter 7, tend to take a backstage role in most of the conversations sketched earlier. This is probably because of the attention given to the core, rather than the wider, NTE.

Equally, it might be interesting to note how these agendas are already painting an interesting degree of dissonance with the most popular issues in city leadership the world over (Rapoport et al, 2019). Those that are perhaps some of the most pressing 'global urban agendas' (Parnell, 2016) usually standing at the heart of municipal government are often poorly intertwined with night-time agendas and issues emerging from the initiatives and debates thus far. For instance, from the 2000s to today, overlaps between climate change action at the city level and night-time governance are virtually absent as an explicit policy mix for most of the cases discussed here. In a similar way, up until the COVID-19 crisis, few explicit policy documents were available internationally on the intersection between health and night-time planning, even despite extensive public health and planning research on this front. This might be an illustration of the relative side-lining of night-time concerns in research and policy. Centrally, it might also be evidence that night-time issues are often poorly connected to the principal matters driving the key agendas of mayors across most cities we depicted. Additionally, besides a few academic studies and, more recently, work on the Global Nightlife Recovery Plan, little work to date has put an emphasis on the *governance* of the night itself. Assessments of the effectiveness, policy trajectory or comparability of night-time governance institutions are almost altogether absent around the world when it comes to local government documentation, with some night-time scholars (Shaw, 2018; Straw, 2018) now calling clearly for more on this front.

Yet, an additional issue that arises here is also that of governance reflexivity and self-assessment. In particular, some of the stories outlined earlier already point to the critical need for night-time governance, whether placed within or outside government, to be regularly at the heart of urban governance more generally – and reflectively so. Regular debate, self-examination and proactive improvement of night-time governance is a characteristic in limited availability across cities the world over. In short, continuity matters. This goes hand in hand with the issue of the legitimacy of the institutions and political-economic infrastructure devised by cities to tackle the night-time. This is essential for those cases whereby night-time governance happens predominantly without local government. Yet, in many cases, it is also an issue of what we could call 'policy embeddedness' for the cases that are within city politics proper. This is to say that lines of clear communication and legitimization are key and needed between external efforts for night-time governance and the government of the place in question. In several of our cases, this has been aided by the presence of a suite of policy and legal groundings for night-time governance realities that are set up by municipal governments themselves. Yet, in turn, it also becomes essential for night-time governance not to be relegated to fleeting advocacy, but rather centred upon the longer-lasting machinery of local government. In order to grasp this more effectively, then, we step here into a more extensive look into a set of case studies to better appreciate the questions of night-time governance, and their trajectories, that emerge internationally.

4

Night-Time Governance Trajectories: A Public–Private Affair?

Introduction

We move here to underline the importance of the urban policy context, its history and trajectory when considering night-time governance cases from around the planet. In order to think through the evolution of the governance of the night in cities with a deeper sense of context, our goal in this first of two in-depth comparative case-study chapters is to stress the value and the institutional positioning of the urban night and the underpinning economic imperatives that drive it in one or another direction. This chapter, then, is once again empirical in nature. It offers more information on the cases of London, Sydney and New York, building on our own work in several of these contexts. In Chapter 5, we move to think of questions of scale, non-governmental imperatives and continuity in the wake of changing political priorities. Overall, these are realities that deal with the issue of night-time governance in very diverse ways and present, in our view, valuable stories of institutionalization to be considered. This is not to privilege a specific set of cities, but rather to highlight the importance of stepping into the lived realities and long-lived pathways that might have cast different governance shapes in places as different as the UK, Australia and the US. Then, in Chapter 5, we speak of Tokyo, Berlin, Valparaiso and Bogota. This allows us to step beyond the summary and bird's-eye-view approach of Chapter 3 to better account for complex private and community interests, how they intersect, and how a mix of public management institutions intersect with each other in the governance of the night-time. We take this point of departure to discuss the public–private relations that began to emerge in Chapter 3 as central to the ways that cities have dealt with the management of what happens after hours. We look at whose interests are represented and what complex urban developmental trajectories are in place. In Chapter 5, then, we highlight how the institutions and the scales depicted in the previous chapters are embedded in local histories. We do so as we seek to offer a more nuanced outline of how these play out through time in major cities around the globe. Practically, we move from the more vignette-based style of Chapter 3 to the longer case studies depicted here. In doing so, we aim to encourage comparative insights in academia and policymaking, offering more specific outlines of how night-time governance has played out in London, New York, Sydney and Melbourne in this chapter, followed by a set of four counterparts (Tokyo, Berlin, Valparaiso and Bogota) in Chapter 5. Our approach is one that seeks to boost the explicit but responsible (that is, wary of context and locality) value of 'comparative gestures' (Robinson, 2011) for night-time scholars and practitioners. In academic terms, this chapter and Chapter 5 are, therefore, aimed at offering a set of 'composing comparisons' (Robinson, 2011) that consider contextual variations among cities by following interconnections and repeated instances in the evolution of urban night-time governance in different contexts. As we reference the literature of night studies, more information about these cases and more suggested readings about their histories and complexities can also be found at the end of the book in the 'Further reading' section.

Governing the NTE in London

As the largest city in the UK and a global capital for culture and the arts, London faces distinct pressures when it comes to night-time management. The questions of what the night is for, and for whom, have been prominent as the city's economy evolved from a dominant manufacturing and industrial centre and capital of the British Empire, to a global financial centre and prominent hub for arts and culture, hospitality, real estate, higher education, and technology (Robin, 2018; Fainstein et al, 2011). This is also an experience that has now inspired both national counterparts like Manchester and international peers like Sydney to strengthen their night-time governance more formally. Yet, what can we glean from the case of London?

The emergence of the NTE as an object for policy

The emergence of the NTE within urban policy discourse in the early 2000s reflects a distinct moment for the regulation of night-time activities. The UK had a history of treating nightlife and evening entertainment as risky activities that were linked to antisocial or untoward behaviours, requiring forms of social control or containment through policing and regulation

(Talbot, 2006). There was no coherent regime for governing the urban night; rather, it was subject to layers of ad hoc policies in the form of the taxation, policing and surveillance, and regulation of licensed venues, established in response to various social or economic concerns (Talbot, 2006). Against this backdrop, the Licensing Act 2003, introduced under the New Labour government, delegated decision-making to local authorities, encouraging local councils to support extended opening hours for licensed venues as a way to instrumentalize the NTE to boost local economic activity. This policy was positioned at the intersection of three drivers of change: culture, economic regeneration, and the licensing and policing of licensed venues (Talbot, 2006). This approach followed the consumption-led model of urban economic development that seeks to foster cultural activities and consumption to stimulate economic growth by attracting 'creative class' workers and innovative business ventures (Gornostaeva and Campbell, 2012).

In many cities, the night has been a fragmented, complex time-space subject to social struggle and contestation (Shaw, 2015). This is no different in London, where the night offered opportunities for self-expression for marginalized groups, including LGBTQI+ nightlife spaces (Campkin and Marshall, 2018), as well as clubs or venues for black and Caribbean populations barred from Central London venues (Talbot, 2004).[1] From the 1990s, the impact of NTE policies on the gentrification and securitization of urban landscapes led to different forms of exclusion by amplifying social inequalities based on race, ethnicity, class, gender, sexuality, age and disability (Hadfield, 2014).

For example, Talbot's (2004) study of NTE policies implemented by a London borough showed how racialized conceptions of violence and culture influenced licensing decisions for local venues. Council officers showed a bias towards venues and events that would attract and cater to white audiences, on the premise that gatherings of young Black people were characterised by a tendency towards violence and represented more of a disorder problem than white events (Talbot, 2004). The Metropolitan Police, who could object to licensing applications on the basis of crime and disorder, also viewed licensed venues popular with black populations as more prone to violence and drug use than dance events, despite evidence showing that drug use was prevalent. This view was internalized by some licensees, such as one who stopped hosting reggae concerts in response to police pressure.

London as a 24-hour city

London's success in stimulating the regeneration of declining areas, and the accompanying growth in property prices, created new challenges for the culture and nightlife sector. The pace of change was stark: between 2007 and 2015, 35 per cent of grass-roots music venues in London closed (GLA, 2015). A report commissioned by the mayor of London attributed the closure of venues to increasing rents and the redevelopment of cultural venues into residential property, as well as higher business rates, inadequate consideration of music venues within local planning policies and a fragmented strategy to manage the NTE (GLA, 2015). A subsequent survey by the Association of Licensed Multiple Retailers (ALMR) showed that the number of clubs in the UK had almost halved between 2005 and 2015.[2] This spurred Mayor of London Boris Johnson to create the Night Time Commission, which conducted a six-month inquiry into the causes of the decline. The creation of this commission reflects the importance of advocacy from industry leaders in the arts and nightlife sectors to prioritize this issue. After current Mayor of London Sadiq Khan assumed office in May 2016, the NTE became a key policy focus. As the mayor and Greater London Authority were preparing to address the wider issues causing the downturn in London's NTE, the public controversy over the attempted closure of London's Fabric nightclub significantly galvanized the agenda. In December 2016, Amy Lamé was appointed as London's first night czar, tasked with championing nightlife across the city. At the same time, Philip Kolvin QC – also the lawyer acting for Fabric – was appointed as chair of the Night Time Commission.

The mayor published his vision for London as a 24-hour city, 'From good night to great night' (GLA, 2017a), in July 2017. The vision reinforced the importance of creative sectors to a city's success and set out the mayor's goals to make London a 'global leader' in the way it planned for nightlife, positing that a 'vibrant nightscape is a mark of cultural status for a global city' and critically important to remain competitive with cities like Paris, New York, Berlin and Tokyo (GLA, 2017c). This vision emphasized that the NTE was not 'just about pubs and clubs', but about making the night 'welcoming and accessible for all' (GLA, 2017b). Since 2016, the governance of London's NTE has proliferated, with a range of appointed representatives or groups, as well as an enterprise zone fund and charters for women's safety and LGBTQ+ venues. Table 1 summarizes the governance of London's NTE.

The revamped Night Time Commission was tasked with producing a report to explain how Londoners use the city between 6 pm and 6 am, drawing together evidence from expert witnesses, commissioners, international research and commissioned research to gather the views of London residents. This report, *Think Night* (London NTC, 2018), was published in November 2018 with ten recommendations for the mayor to implement. *Think Night* redefined the 24-hour city, with a stronger focus on quality of life, as well as cultural and economic activities, highlighting that 1.6 million Londoners regularly work at night, and two thirds of the population use the night for errands, shopping and socializing (GLA, 2018a).

Table 1: Governance of the NTE in London

Positions or groups appointed	
Night Czar	Amy Lamé
Night Time Commission	Chaired by Philip Kolvin QC (2016–18) Kate Nicholls, Chief Executive Officer, UK Hospitality (2018–current)
Night Time Champions Network	Champions within London's 32 borough councils
Late Night Transport Working Group	Amy Lamé and staff from Transport for London, the Greater London Authority and London Underground
Funding mechanisms and charters	
Night Time Enterprise Zone Fund	Pilot fund for borough councils to develop projects to test extended opening hours or other activities
Women's Night Safety Charter	Charter with seven pledges for organizations to sign up to in order to improve safety for women at night (393 signatories)
LGBTQ+ Venues Charter	Charter with five pledges for developers, venues and pubs to support LGBTQ+ venues (29 signatories)

It also asserted the importance of decentralized approaches to governing the NTE, with borough-level strategies to allow each of the city's 32 boroughs to shape their strategy to local needs. The recommendations set out for the mayor are summarized in Table 2.

Three controversies across London's NTE

To understand the hybrid of public and private interests that shape the governance of London's NTE, three key controversies that emerged between 2016 and 2018 illustrate the conflicting interests and fragmentation of powers that predominate in London.

Introduction of restrictions on opening hours in the London borough of Hackney

The introduction of restrictions on the opening hours for new licensed venues in the London borough of Hackney in mid-2018 spurred strong opposition from local operators and prominent figures in the entertainment and hospital sectors. This controversy is a notable example to illustrate the tensions between night-time operators, local councils and residents, as well as

Table 2: Recommendations from London's Night Time Commission (2018)

1. Introduce a 'night test' for new policies to rate their impact on London's culture, sociability, well-being and economy at night	2. Produce night-time guidance for boroughs to develop holistic local strategies
3. Set up a London Night Time Data Observatory with a central hub of data and analytics	4. Produce an annual report about London at night, with metrics to report on progress against the recommendations and vision
5. Establish a Night Time Enterprise Zone Fund	6. Commission research to establish the case for longer opening hours across London
7. Establish new partnerships across London to improve safety, reduce violence and make London welcoming for everyone at night	8. Develop guidance for boroughs, landowners and developers to create welcoming, vibrant and safe public spaces
9. Set up a Late Night Transport Working Group to ensure that workers, visitors and customers can travel quickly and safely at night	10. Extend the remit of London & Partners[a] to promote London's night-time offer to Londoners

Note: [a] London's international trade, investment and promotion agency.

the fragmented governance between local authorities and appointed leaders working across Greater London.

Hackney is a salient case to examine the tension between thriving nightlife and a good night's sleep for Londoners. While the number of pubs across London declined by 25 per cent between 2001 and 2016 (GLA, 2017b), Hackney bucked this trend as the only borough not to see a decline – but rather a 3 per cent increase – in the number of pubs. This statistic points to the wider transformation of the borough from a poorly connected and deprived area to one of the city's most desirable areas for nightlife and retail shopping (Lagadic, 2019). In July 2018, Hackney Council voted to make any new pubs, clubs and bars in Dalston and Shoreditch close at 11 pm on weekdays and midnight on the weekend. This prevented new all-night venues from opening in these areas, effectively capping the number of late-night venues in Dalston and Shoreditch.

Campaign group We Love Hackney (WLH) raised funds to launch a legal challenge against the council's decision and received permission for a judicial review of the decision in early 2019 (Gelder, 2019). WLH argued that the council's decision went against the views of local residents, since 84 per cent of consultation respondents disagreed with the new core hours (Hackney Council, 2018). The group argued that while the council claimed to be balancing the NTE's growth with amenity for local residents, the policy change was instead 'a gift to big corporates.... By forcing up the value of a licence, they will leave an area like Shoreditch as sterile and soulless as Leicester Square, pushing out anyone with deep pockets' (WLH, 2018). WLH was subsequently forced to abandon the hearing in June 2019 after their bid for a cost-capping order to limit their financial liability was rejected. The judge ruled that the order was not appropriate for a case backed by 'wealthy individuals who have a commercial interest in the litigation' (Sheridan, 2019). The contestation over Hackney's restrictions on liquor licensing shows the complex landscape of stakeholder interests involved in the NTE. While the council claimed that they had sought to strike a balance between the local economy and amenity for residents, campaign groups composed of residents, local business owners and entrepreneurs claimed that the council's decision instead benefitted corporate interests and property developers. The presence of commercial interests within WLH itself further complicated the question of whose interests were represented by the council and the campaign group.

Attempted closure of Fabric nightclub

The London borough of Islington's decision to shut down one of London's most prominent nightclubs, Fabric, marked a flashpoint for the governance of the NTE. The Metropolitan Police asked Islington Council to shut down the nightclub in September 2016 after a series of drug-related deaths at the venue in the preceding years (Coldwell, 2016). Since Fabric was an internationally renowned nightclub, this decision was interpreted in the media as a symbol of the demise of London's NTE. The move to revoke the club's licence received heavy media scrutiny and strong public opposition. Mayor Sadiq Khan issued a public statement to express his disappointment with the outcome, attributing this case to the wider decline of 'world-class nightlife' in London (Khan, 2016).

Fabric launched a fundraising campaign to appeal the decision in court; however, it was resolved before the scheduled hearing after negotiation between the nightclub, Islington Council and the Metropolitan Police led to an agreement to reinstate the licence (Garcia, 2018). This reversal was publicly supported by London's new Night Czar Amy Lamé and Mayor Sadiq Khan, signalling the wider symbolic importance of Fabric to London's NTE (Nicholson, 2016).

The decision to close Fabric was ostensibly driven by health-and-safety risks at the venue; however, there was contestation about the possible underlying motives for the decision. Some venue managers claimed that there was a correlation between complaints from local residents and the level of scrutiny from the policy (Garcia, 2018). This, in turn, was interpreted by stakeholders in the NTE as the selective application of drugs policing in areas where residents opposed 'non-illegal nuisances' and 'undesirable groups' (Garcia, 2018). These uncertainties reflect a crucial challenge of governing the NTE, as tensions between local amenity and the economic and cultural successes of nightlife are resolved at the discretion of local government or policing bodies, spurring further contestation from NTE stakeholders or residents who feel that their interests are not considered.

Improving the transport offering for Londoners at night

Transport was a key policy intervention to support the NTE, for example, with the introduction of London's Night Tube in August 2016. The Night Tube was declared a success in terms of attracting riders, with ridership growing to 8.7 million in 2018 (GLA, 2018b). However, concerns were raised over a 30 per cent increase in reported violent crime and sexual assault on night services between 2018 and 2019, despite the introduction of additional transport police for the Night Tube (Boscia, 2019). The lack of affordable and frequent transport options for night-time workers was also highlighted as a shortcoming in the Night Tube policy (Smeds et al, 2020; Kolioulis, 2018). However, the Night Tube only operates on selected lines, and substantial cuts to public transport funding in recent years have undermined Transport for London's (TfL's) wider efforts to improve transport provision at night. In 2015, the central government opted to remove TfL's £700 million annual subsidy, requiring the transport network to cover all of its costs through fares, charges and commercial activities (Sullivan and Pickard, 2015). In conjunction with Mayor Sadiq Khan's commitments to freeze fares, this created a substantial financial shortfall for TfL.

Prior to the COVID-19 pandemic, TfL had already reduced service frequency or coverage across a number of routes (Hoscik, 2018). Night buses, in particular, were affected (Walker, 2018), as they are often loss-making due to lower patronage. A further factor that compounded TfL's financial challenges was the increase in the use of ride-hailing services, such as Uber, ViaVan, Bolt and Kapten. These alternatives have been identified as a driver of lower public transport usage, particularly for trips at night (Bray and Bellamy, 2019). Uber's licence to operate in London has been revoked twice by TfL since it entered the city in 2012 following concerns over fraudulent use of the platform by drivers and allegations of sexual assault (Browne, 2020a). The potential cost to the NTE was used to oppose this decision, with bars and restaurants publicly criticizing TfL's choice, claiming that it would reduce customer numbers and spending (O'Mahony and Orrell, 2017). However, in both cases, Uber appealed the decision successfully, and the service is still operating (Browne, 2020b). This outcome left London with declining public transport revenue, service coverage and patronage, as well as a proliferation of rideshare companies operating in competition with the dominant platform, Uber.

The decision by the central government to remove TfL's annual operating subsidy, and London's lack of control over its public transport funding, show how ambitions to improve transport accessibility at night are significantly constrained. The political tensions between the Conservative-led central government and Labour mayor of London intersect with the city's NTE policies, limiting funding needed to expand night bus and tube services to meet transport needs across the city.

Overall, the governance of the NTE in London shows a distinct departure from previous approaches that focused narrowly on culture as a source of economic development and regeneration. The policy discourse since 2016 recasts the NTE as a means of improving inclusivity and creative industries, as well as stimulating economic activity. The three controversies reviewed show the unresolved tensions between the goals of inclusivity and creative activities, as well as the local economy. Governance arrangements feature overlapping responsibilities to foster and champion the NTE, which can align effectively, as in the case of the Fabric nightclub, but also have unclear boundaries. While the direct control of licensing and public spaces is held by local authorities, and the central government retains the ability to restrict transport funding, London's mayor and appointed officials, such as the night czar and Night Time Commission, utilize their convening power to advocate for, and build public support behind, the NTE agenda.

Regulating the city that never sleeps

The 'city that never sleeps', as the famous lyrics from the main theme of Martin Scorsese's New York, New York memorably put it, is an obvious candidate to international attention when speaking of the NTE. New York's vibrant nightlife industry, as well as subcultures, crime scenes and atmospheres, have been chronicled time and time again in research and media, and not unfairly. If New York's nightlife industry represented an estimated US$9.7 billion of economic activity in 2004, with US$2.6 billion in wages and 95,500 jobs, this has grown exponentially in a decade. As of the latest NYC's Nightlife Economy report (New York City Government, 2019), the nightlife industry supported 299,000 jobs, with US$13.1 billion in employee compensation and US$35.1 billion in total economic output. This annual economic impact also yielded US$697 million in tax revenue for the city. How has a city of comparable size (8.3 million people) and international visibility to London managed this growth and its associated challenges?

At present, nightlife governance is centred onto two main bodies, the Office of Nightlife and its Nightlife Advisory Board, both part of the Mayor's

Office of Media and Entertainment (MOME), and thus under New York City's mayoral purview, similar to London, especially in connection to the deputy mayor for housing and economic development. Yet, it took quite a while for New York City to set up a formal structure for nightlife governance. It was not until September 2017 that legislation establishing the Office of Nightlife and Advisory Board was signed by the mayor. Nonetheless, night-time politics and policy are no novelty in the city. Rather, today's evolution towards a more formalized Office of Nightlife has its roots in early 20th-century regulation and a near-century-long dispute over the control of the Big Apple's NTE.

The famous 'Cabaret Law' that is at the heart of this story was, in fact, enacted by the then Committee on Local Laws in 1926 to improve neighbourhood safety at night and reduce noises by prohibiting musical entertainment, including singing and dancing, without a licence. This typically resulted in high complexities for small business owners or non-profit art communities to acquire operating licences, especially in the eyes of critics, who tagged the law as racist, homophobic and authoritarian over numerous decades. Yet, in turn, the strictness of these regulations led to both an expanding, if not a thriving, 'underground' night-time scene and the development of lobbying coalitions of either business owners or (and at times with) community groups.

Much of the story of urban night-time governance in New York, then, is one of local industry associations and municipal politics beyond, against and for a shift in council regulations. In the late 1980s, the New York Cabaret Association (NYCA) was formed, focusing on operating hours and zones for dance clubs (Hae, 2012). In 1998, the NYCA changed its name to the New York Nightlife Association (NYNA), which became a strong advocate in making a case for the night in the city. The NYNA, for instance, published a report revealing the NTE value for New York City in 2004, which then not only led to the release of nightlife best practices to guide safety issues for nightlife establishments through collaborative partnerships with the New York Police Department (NYPD), but also had significant influence on economic policymaking (Hae, 2011) and the eventual launch of the Office of Nightlife. Similarly, the Hospitality Alliance emerged as an influential lobby, as did several associations like Legalize Dance NYC (LDNYC) and the NYC Artist Coalition. In the 1980s, the Cabaret Law was tightened because the city, led by Mayor Ed Koch, focused on tourism and real estate revenues at the cost of nightlife growth. This is a period when, for instance, bodies like Local 802, the national musicians' union, repeatedly challenged the law's discrimination against live music and social dancing – not least in court. A key legal milestone in these efforts was the 1988 judgment in *Chiasson vs NYC*, when Local 802 supported the overturning of the law that required three performers (or instrument types) on one stage to legalize dancing. In this often-adversarial environment between administrations and civil society/ business, the existence of several public–private relations stresses, once again, that urban night-time governance happens very much 'inside-out' of a municipal structure. For instance, a fundamental collaboration established by the NYPD and Hospitality Alliance, a peak industry association with deep interest in the Big Apple's nightlife, led to the issuing of best practice guidelines for nightlife establishments in 2018.

These governance relations, however, also underscore that in municipal politics, public–private linkages are not always collaborative, even between the same actors, and that partnerships might shift to adversarial linkages. The 2018 *Best Practice for Nightlife* report and the NYPD's collaboration with the city's Hospitality Alliance is, in this sense, more of a culmination of a long battle between these sectors that reached its tipping point in the late 1990s. The Cabaret Law remained relatively dormant until the Giuliani administration (1994–2001), when it was 'dusted off' and used as a mechanism to crack down on nightlife, often leading to venue closures and displacing many realities, very similar to the case of London, especially when it comes to more vulnerable groups. The prompt for change came again from sustained community activism and, at the same time, NTE business pressures. In the late 2010s, several town hall meetings by these actors in iconic venues like the Market Hotel (following a police raid in October 2016) focused on repealing the Cabaret Law. This push eventually gathered momentum with some New York City Council members. This movement was mainly fronted by 27th District Democratic Councillor Rafael Espinal, who introduced and passed the 2017 bill repealing the law and leading to the establishment of the Office of Nightlife. In March 2018, this was followed by the appointment of Ariel Palitz as Senior Executive Director of the Office of Nightlife by the mayor, informally the 'night mayor' of New York City. The Office of Nightlife and executive director have also been supported by the launch of a complementary, newly formed, all-volunteer, 14-member independent body to advise the mayor and the City Council on issues affecting the nightlife industry. This Nightlife Advisory Board is charged with making recommendations on ways to improve regulations and policies that impact nightlife establishments, in a similar set-up to London, but still lacks the more specific approach of taskforce and working groups of the British capital. Nonetheless, the story of New York speaks to the British case, both in terms of the importance of public–private relations and confrontations in the shaping of the governance of the urban night, and in terms of the underpinning histories of municipal politics that can lead to the establishment of key nightlife policymaking bodies like the Office of Nightlife in New York City or the night czar in London.

Among night-time interests: institutionalizing the NTE in Sydney

For over a decade now, Sydney has recognized the fact that, as the City Council puts it, the NTE is 'critical to the city's future'. The leadership of the city has embraced night-time activity to quite some degree. Albeit still centred on 'core NTE' business, this approach has nonetheless progressively been expanding into areas other than the entertainment, culture and tourism industries. This is a case whereby the NTE has been institutionalized not only across both governance and regulation, but also in the views of the business sector. This is also a case that (as we outline below) is something starkly different from Sydney's national 'rival', Melbourne, which, in turn, has only just recently moved in a similar direction. Yet, this NTE-focused leadership is also a case that underlines continuing tensions in this process of institutionalization of the night-time in urban politics, stressing how a multitude of interests are at stake when seeking to make a mark as a night-time-oriented city.

A history of regulation

The city of Sydney, which occupies the core Central Business District (CBD) of the 10,000 km² Greater Sydney conurbation and houses most of its internationally renowned landmarks, has time and time again stressed the centrality of the NTE to its growth. The case for the night has been repeatedly articulated by the authorities and business sector, for instance, by recently stressing that the NTE generates upwards of AU$4 billion in revenue each year and is the most concentrated in the country. Yet, in turn, this flurry of night-time activity is caught in between a multitude of interests and complex agendas that contrast and clash around Sydney's night-time. This is not a unique reality in Sydney's greater 'neighbourhood'. Australia, in fact, has a solid track record of similar initiatives taken by secondary cities across the country, ranging from Newcastle, the Gold Coast and Canberra, to Ballarat, Hobart and the city of Yarra. Of course, this expansion of the NTE as an object of business and policy attention has not been free from critique. Colleagues in Sydney and Perth have already noted that night-time council policies across Australia might have been 'gentrifying the night', with some resulting in the 'pricing out' of communities from nightlife precincts across metropolitan Australia, rather than promoting economic vitality (see Sisson and Maginn, 2018). Therefore, in practice, the NTE in Australia has already been recognized as heavily political, at least by scholars. What is clear in the recent history of the NTE in Sydney is that the governance of the urban night is tightly intertwined with complex sets of local and regional regulation, legislation and policymaking – and, conversely, that these are steeped in urban governance struggles in and about the city. As Australian scholarship has already highlighted (Beer, 2011), there is certainly a long history of night-time challenges and issues affecting the way Sydney has developed through the years from a settler colony to today's so-called 'global city' status. A quick excursus through the last decade or so of NTE policymaking affecting the specific reality of the city of Sydney is telling here. There are a vast number of laws and legislative reviews that have impinged on the development of the NTE in the city. For instance, the early 2000s witnessed extensive policy, business and academic debate surrounding the issue of managing the impact of late-night trading or, more broadly, the management of how an expanding NTE related to the needs and problems of residents. This is where, for instance, the city of Sydney's (2007) *Late Night Trading Premises Development Control Plan* was introduced hand in hand with the state government's Liquor Act 2007, which was aimed at controlling and providing oversight over alcohol consumption as a source of insecurity at night-time. Similar connections have peppered the history of Sydney's night-time governance.

This is, of course, a reality that is repeating itself nearly a decade later, with reviews from the local government and community fronts for specifically liquor, gaming and small bars calling for a rethinking of the New South Wales government's liquor restrictions and legislation around small bars, as well as of licensing and policing of the city at night-time. While these are well-rehearsed NTE themes in many of the case studies that we have already come across, it is also important to underscore how in parallel to such a process, as we noted earlier, the city of Sydney has progressively engaged in the development of a night-time governance infrastructure made up of strategies and policies to control and steer this expanding NTE reality. Yet, at the same time, this takes place in the wake of a state government and a business community also repeatedly entering into the picture, providing pushes and pulls from all scales and directions of the political spectrum towards how Sydney's urban night-time governance has evolved. For instance, in October 2011, and following on from the 2008 *Sustainable Sydney 2030* strategy (Sydney, 2011), the council embarked on a series of citizen consultations and business engagements to develop an explicit plan for the future direction of the city at night. This started with a discussion paper titled 'Open Sydney' (Sydney, 2011), which was then to become an actual plan two years later in 2013. Yet, this process also continued through both conversation and drawing extensively on the business community and consultants as key research informants for the city. For example, this was the case with a late-night management areas research programme in December 2013 that set much of the tone for the council's stance, as well as with a variety of other research reports, such as a number of iterations of work to define the shape and impact of the Australian NTE in 2015, 2018 and 2019 by the Council of Capital Cities Lord Mayor (CCCLM), which has itself been an important network governance driver for the city of Sydney to further intertwine its local development with other major Australian cities.

A clash of scales

The concurrent interests of local governments, networks of municipalities, the state government, businesses and many other actors speaks volumes to the multiplicity of scales at play in the governance of Sydney's NTE. Importantly, these diverse spatial orientations bring about the possibility of contrast and confrontation taking place 'asymmetrically' between the local, regional and other scales of urban governance – a dimension that the case of Sydney could help us unravel more systematically.

An example of this is the Sydney 'lockout laws' introduced by the government of New South Wales in the early months of 2014, explicitly orienting action towards limiting alcohol-related crime and questions of security across the metropolitan area, and effectively shutting down NTE venues, especially when it came to the Sydney CBD entertainment precinct (Lee et al, 2020). Provisions of the lockout laws have been the object of fierce local debate, both by night-time industry associations and with continuing critique by the city's lord mayor, including repeated engagements and reviews eventually occurring in front of the state parliament (Homan, 2019). The laws were eventually scrapped almost in their entirety in the early months of 2020. While, of course, much can be told about the sub-national politics surrounding a case like this, an interesting point of note for our perhaps shorter excursus here is that two critical elements in turning the state's stance on and support for the laws, and eventually their demise, were those of evidence production and economic cost–benefit analyses. Practically, this means that the assertion that the laws were predominantly oriented towards limiting alcohol-related violence and crime was fast met throughout much of the second half of the 2010s with the sustained production of studies oriented towards understanding how the core NTE operates in Sydney around issues such as footfall, perceived safety and security. Indeed, this also contributed to a wider and growing consensus about making what we could call a 'case for the night', illustrating the size of the NTE contribution to the state's overall revenue and the necessity to support the NTE as a growing element in the longer-term development of the city, further strengthened by the downturn brought about by the COVID-19 crisis. These concerns emerge from the rapid emergence of the NTE over the past three decades. As research has highlighted, this has also affected the precarity and complex positioning of night-time workers: Australia and, indeed, Sydney have witnessed substantial changes in the structure of work that have had clear ramifications for the leisure industry, including the proliferation of part-time and service-oriented labour (Rowe and Lynch, 2012).

In turn, this is an example of how the scalar dimension of urban governance comes into play even more explicitly. For example, in response to the impact of the COVID-19 crisis and a perceived still poor public recognition of the value of the NTE across the city, the state government launched an explicit plan to bolster the 24-hour capacity of the Greater Sydney region at the end of 2019. The *Greater Sydney 24-hour Economy Strategy* (New South Wales Government, 2020) also includes continuing transformation in the institutional dimension of what the governance of the urban night looks like in Sydney. The 24-hour economy plan explicitly aims to: appoint a 'coordinator general' for Greater Sydney's 24-hour economy; establish a 24-hour economy 'acceleration programme' for local councils (not just the city of Sydney); and directly put in place recognition systems like a 'night-time hub certification programme' to highlight core NTE areas of the metropolitan area. As quite explicitly noted in the strategy, this is partly about: changing narratives and not financing; not just marketing, but also rebalancing across the metropolitan area; pushing towards a wider metropolitan conversation beyond the role of city of Sydney; and seeking to produce this single view of existing 24-hour hubs, as well as seeding potential new ones.

Institutionalizing the 24-hour city

The success of the NTE in the work of the city of Sydney is not just the result of regulation, clashes on nightlife and economic returns (Wadds, 2020). The city also explicitly underscores how central the functioning of its night-time activities is to the overall sustainability of Sydney, repeatedly tackling and engaging with questions of safety, crime and resilience, and, more recently, takings clearer positions towards inequality at night-time. Much of this is now captured in a well-known strategic plan launched in 2013 called 'Open Sydney' (Sydney, 2011), aimed at setting the course of the city's NTE between 2013 and 2030. Yet, the management of the night in the city of Sydney goes well beyond the local government's area vision for the long-term development of Sydney's night-time. The council has developed a variety of mechanisms for funding and supporting night-time activities, such as night-time diversification grants for new events and initiatives that explicitly target driving customers to the city in the evening, as well as their Safe Space programme, dedicated to an explicit focus on young people, and late-night trading provisions for live music and performance venues. Further, as a clear and tangible example of the operation of NTE policy mobility across continents, the city hosted a series of independent forums called 'Global Cities After Dark', first held in 2017, then 2018 and 2019, and co-organized by VibeLab and local music entrepreneurs, with participation of the city of Sydney. These 'night culture forums' have been hosting a variety of key figures in NTE advocacy and action, many of which have made an international mark and are chronicled already in several of the case studies in Chapter 3. Fittingly, 'Global Cities After Dark' also emerged as linked to an initiative funded through a so-called 'knowledge exchange grant', aimed at connecting the city of Sydney with circuits of urban innovation and policy experimentation. This is an activity that the council is well renowned for internationally. For instance, it has played a relatively proactive role in the C40 Cities climate leadership group of the world's major metropolises tackling climate change since 2008 and in the 100 Resilient Cities Initiative launched by the Rockefeller Foundation in 2013. The NTE is no different on this front. Overall, leadership for the NTE has had alternate successes in the apparatus of government of the city of Sydney. Originally tasked explicitly as a portfolio for a deputy mayor role, it is now mainly pivoted on the figure of a night-time manager, who, in turn, has been behind the development of the 'Open Sydney' plan and networking through summits and exchanges.

The case of Sydney speaks clearly to the continuing purchase of the 24/7 interpretation (Crary, 2013) of the NTE amid governmental and business elites (Wolifson, 2018). Just like in the case of London First, the main business leadership organization of the city, the Committee for Sydney has been repeatedly pushing in this direction. For instance, the committee established a purpose-specific Sydney Night Time Economy Commission in May 2017, which included input from 40 private, public and civic sector organizations. The result of the commission emerged in 2018 through an aptly titled *Sydney as a 24-hour City* report (Committee for Sydney, 2018) – a call to action for local policymakers across the whole of the Greater Sydney area to embrace this line of thinking. This is an approach oriented towards not just putting Sydney's NTE narrative side by side with national rivals (that is, Melbourne), but also pushing for policy mobility and competitiveness rationales with the likes of London, Hong Kong and other 'global cities'. Overall, then, this underscores a networked and internationalist approach underpinning the governance of the urban night in the city of Sydney, perhaps, to some degree, different from the relatively localized and less prominently articulated strategic vision in the neighbouring case of the city of Melbourne. Sydney has predominantly been at the forefront of policymaking discussion and, indeed, clash with other governmental scales, differently but perhaps now more convergingly with the nearby case of Melbourne.

Night-time governance is now high on the cards in both cities – more so that it has been for quite a while.

Same country, opposite stories?

In Australia, the NTE has had increasing purchase on local policymakers. CCCLM, as the association of capital cities, has a dedicated working group on this, and many local authorities, not just the major ones, have developed plans and projects in this area. One would, then, almost expect the national rivalry between the country's two pre-eminent cities, Sydney and Melbourne, to have something to do with the NTE, at least to some degree. Yet, this is not quite the story. In Melbourne, NTE leadership has predominantly emerged from the private sector, especially that coalescing around night-time venues, culture and entertainment industries. While Sydney explicitly sanctioned the NTE as a key activity of the council and promoted network exchanges such as the 'Global Cities After Dark' conference, Melbourne has seen similar events emerge from outside local government. This is the case, for example, of the '24 Hour Cities Victorian Night Time Economy' summit in 2018, emerging predominantly from actors such as not-for-profit Music Victoria. While many of these activities are not necessarily at odds with the city council and are often sanctioned through alignment with and participation in council activities, such as the Melbourne Music Week or the Melbourne Knowledge Week, it would be hard to argue that the city of Melbourne has played a leadership role in urban night-time governance. Mentions of night-time management issues were scant across the city's key strategies and policies. A 2008 '24-hour city' council policy had lain relatively dormant for quite some time as mayors changed, while 'next door' councils like the city of Yarra had been developing NTE reviews and schemes. The city administration run a relatively successful and long-lived (25 years) Licensee Forum, gathering a number of key night operator associations and focused on late-night entertainment precincts and safe night-time environments. However, this has not been coupled with a broader NTE management role and remit across other areas of the council. Some limited state-level initiatives part-filled this gap, for instance, with the rollout of a Night Network of late-night transport by Public Transport Victoria (PTV) in 2016, covering six tram lines, 21 bus routes and four regional coaches, and extending radially from the city of Melbourne across Greater Melbourne. Likewise, to date, broad initiative for explicit policy action and reform has mainly remained within the state government remit, very often prompted by non-governmental initiatives by business and community actors, for instance, like Music Victoria. For example, this is the case of the much-chronicled 2014 adoption of the 'Agent of Change' principle in planning law to protect nightlife venues and drive developer action (a globally renowned approach that we detail in more depth in Chapter 5).

Yet, contrary to the experience of New South Wales, the state government of Victoria has taken limited steps in the direction of night management. Even in the wake of the early impacts of COVID-19, as New South Wales (2020) launched the *Sydney 24-hour Economy Strategy*, Melbourne and Victoria seemed to be lagging.

Over the last two decades, these efforts outside council (or state government) processes have typically coincided with explicit advocacy emerging from the non-governmental side of the Melbourne story, rather than being explicitly on the agenda of subsequent lord mayors of the city of Melbourne. This is not to say that Victoria is void of efforts that might, to some degree, be aligned with the city of Sydney's progress. Interestingly, in fact, the Victorian capital has perhaps been surrounded by a number of smaller and less internationally renowned councils that have nevertheless led on NTE thinking much more explicitly than Melbourne itself. This is the case, for instance, of adjoining Yarra City Council, which has issued a variety of NTE discussion papers, and regional Victorian realities like the city of Ballarat, which undertook explicit studies of what it called the 'right to the night' across its local government area. This antipodean comparison introduces not so much a greatly chronicled national rivalry between the two thriving global cities, but rather a snapshot of how differently institutionalized the NTE might be. This is illustrated to be the case even in relatively similar urban governance and economic contexts. See Sydney through the prism of its comparison with Melbourne testifies to a relatively extensive story of regulation, strategy making and recognition of the potential (and challenges) of the city after dark.

Despite being an international hub well known for its arts and culture scene, hospitality business, and global city outlook, Melbourne had been relatively silent on night-time planning, policy and politics over the past few years. Mentions of night-time management issues were scant across the city's key strategies and policies, a 2008 '24-hour city' council approach had lain dormant for quite some time as mayors changed, while 'next door', the city of Sydney and its state of New South Wales had been rolling out night-time strategies, portfolios and state-wide plans. Even in the wake of the early impacts of COVID-19, as New South Wales launched a 24-hour-economy policy for Sydney, Melbourne seemed to be lagging behind. Then, in the midst of what has been flagged as one of the strictest, seven-month-long lockdowns around the world, the night-time took centre stage in the city. While Melbourne's state of Victoria sluggishly rolled out a AU$40 million Night Time Business Economy Support Initiative, the debate on how to manage not just the after hours, but explicitly its recovery through COVID-19, became a hot issue in the November 2020 mayoral election that saw Sally Capp being reconfirmed as lord mayor. On Capp's ticket, the appointment of a night mayor, now in the works, was a key proposal for the city's businesses to rally behind. At the same time, other party contenders touted night-time governance ideas of all sorts, from neighbourhood festivals and 'white night' festivals (holding hospitality late at night), to homeless support projects, night czars and commissions, to directly importing New York City's model of the Office of Nightlife.

This might, in fact, highlight some potentially convergent role played by the impact of the 2020 crisis, bringing us to some alignment in policy direction, but it also underscores different ways of interpreting the night and the near-full gamut of night-time advocates and actors that might be at play when we speak of the governance of the urban night. While the candidate councillor slated to be appointed night mayor was not elected, resulting, at least temporarily, in a shelving of the idea, the new council and the administration of the city of Melbourne have now taken up more explicitly the goal to recognize and manage the city's NTE. The NTE has thus been identified in council's annual plan as part of a major initiative for 2020–21, to be led by the Economic Development branch, within the context of developing a broader economic development strategy for the city. A 'focus on the night time economy' is explicitly highlighted in the plan to 'support economic growth during the COVID-19 recovery period', as well as calls to 'explore appropriate support for consumer groups, trader groups and business precincts, [and the] activation of vacant retail premises'. Melbourne's NTE has been significantly impacted by COVID-19. The scale and mix of the NTE are a key part of Melbourne's economic recovery, and creating a welcoming and safe environment for everyone is a key priority. In December 2019, the newly elected city council recognized the impact of the crisis on the NTE and the 'need for priority action'. The council supported a proposal to establish a Night Time Economy Advisory Committee. The advisory committee kicked off in 2021 to provide the administration and council with strategic advice on policy and issues associated with reviving Melbourne's NTE, potentially moving Melbourne more in the direction of Sydney. It also allowed renowned Cherry Bar nightclub-owner James Young, who had lost his bid for selection as the 'night mayor' candidate on Lord Mayor Sally Capp's ticket, to be informally touted as Melbourne's new 'night chairman'. As the committee takes its first steps towards reviving the NTE into Melbourne's headlines after a hiatus since the 2005 24-hour policy, these moves seem to be paralleled across the country's major capitals. Topically for our previous case study, the city of Sydney has also ventured into formalizing a similar set-up: as of late 2018, it has launched a Nightlife and Creative Sector Advisory Panel formed by 15 experts (Sydney 2020), explicitly including youth voices (aged under 30) and, as with Melbourne, the recognition of key local academic experts on night-time governance. Importantly, the panel's justification is once again both economic and networked, stressing that it aims to be similar to models already operating in other global cities, such as Amsterdam, Berlin, London and New York. Overall, then, the comparison with Melbourne, even when inter-referenced with other NTE experiences overseas, stresses the underlying importance of municipal politics and localized interests in charting the developmental trajectory of how the NTE is managed in contexts like our antipodean duo.

Notes

[1] Especially through the 'colour bar' imposed in venues in London's West End, refusing service to non-white diners.

[2] The number of clubs dropped from 3,144 in 2005 to 1,733 in 2015.

5

Night-Time Governance Trajectories: The Importance of Scale and Politics

Introduction

The trajectories of night-time governance presented in Chapter 4 speak to the need to understand the institutionalization of how we manage the NTE within the broader context of urban governance. Numerous factors that are often sidelined in much of the practice, and some of the literature, stand out already. Questions of scales of governance, political-economic continuity, embeddedness of the NTE into a progressively 24/7 society (Crary, 2013) and contestation and inequalities at night all stand out as key learnings from the stories of Sydney and London, and their Melbourne and New York counterparts, sketched out in Chapter 4.

We move here, then, to look in more depth into these themes, introducing four more case studies: those of Tokyo in Japan, Berlin in Germany, Valparaiso in Chile and Bogota in Colombia. In doing so, we stress the necessity of paying closer attention to the scalar depth of night-time governance and the 'bottom-up' attention for the NTE that might emerge, as the Tokyo story tells us, in the absence of strong government action. Yet, to counterbalance this view, we also spotlight the challenges that might emerge from the opposite, as in Valparaiso, where local government buy-in to the NTE might not have translated directly into action and continuity (24horas.cl, 2017). In between these two cases is Berlin, a case that stresses further how the non-governmental realm is still a critical one for night-time action, and how the action of committees or associations should not be underplayed due to their capacity to animate night-time governance. We also provide a comparative insight stemming from Bogota, which illustrates how cities' night-time policies can evolve significantly from restrictive towards more enabling regulations in the wake of changing social, economic and political priorities. Overall, then, we also seek to gesture explicitly to the need to decentre stories of the night-time beyond the much-discussed 'West' (whatever that unspecific geographical marker might mean) and account for stories and histories hailing from different 'Eastern' and 'Southern' experiences. An important lesson that stands out to us from this additional mix of cases is that of the necessity to both situate and attend to the broader urban politics that the NTE unfolds in, while keeping a close eye on the capacity of non-governmental realities to drive the trajectory of night-time governance.

For whom and from where? Tokyo's nights from below

The current emphasis on the role of 'night mayors' has brought NTE issues to the fore in urban policy worldwide. Yet, this might have also run the risk of biasing the conversation about the governance of the night-time towards a specific layer of government and initiatives that might, internationally, not be as common as some media attention might suggest. As we have already argued throughout the book, that is often the case for non-Western examples of night-time governance. On the contrary, there might be some great value in including alternative geographical perspectives on the night-time question. These can allow us to push towards a more complex landscape of NTE action and, as the stories of London and Sydney have begun sketching, a more 'multi-scalar' view of the urban governance of what happens after hours. This calls upon both practitioners and scholars to engage with cultures other than those represented by the popularly chronicled European and North American examples. The experience of Tokyo can teach us valuable viewpoints. As cases like Amsterdam, San Francisco and New York already hint at, the story of urban governance needs to be read from a few possible angles – and even in one of the largest megacities on the planet, that might mean going 'down' to the neighbourhood and community levels, as well as beyond the formalized action of local and metropolitan governments. This might be even more poignant if we consider a case that, like Tokyo, presents us with a relative absence of government action, leaving much of the NTE initiative to non-governmental or locally organized entities. Before we jump into this consideration, let us begin with the Japanese capital and its long-standing history of nightlife.

Long tradition, recent history?

Tokyo is famous for its dazzling lights and night-time vitality, characterized by efficient 24-hour services since at least the 1980s. The sprawl of the city (and much of the other major Japanese urban hubs) has an interesting origin, not only in attending to the general populace, but also tightly intertwined with the 20th-century emergence of the figure of the white-collar *sarari man* ('salaryman') worker from large business corporations and the expanding bureaucracy, and with the sprawling business of *izakaya* bars (居酒屋), first very much family-run, but now increasingly part of a commercialized culture across the country (Futamura and Sugiyama, 2018). Along with this evolved a complex scene of cultural economies, relatively 'underground' movements and experimental realities, and continuous complication between regulators, the police and alternatively emerging sub-economies of all sorts, whose troubled relations with government were often tested in Tokyo's neighbourhoods like Shinjuku. While a discussion of this century-long history of NTE policymaking could occupy a chapter of its own, a key point is critical here: there has been a long tradition of night-time experimentation and governance, often informal, in the Japanese capital – and one that is as long as, if not in many cases longer than, many of the other case studies at hand here.

However, the NTE has not been discussed extensively in Tokyo's municipal and regional politics, as well as in academic work, until quite recently. This perhaps has its present-day origins in the 2015 nationwide relaxing of clubbing laws, which made more night entertainment activities possible after hours. In this context, Tokyo's conversation on the night-time has certainly peaked in the last few years and seems to be on an upward trajectory. Central in the support by governmental and business sectors has been the attention to tourism and the entertainment sector as essential to economic development in the Japanese capital (Kadokura, 2007). For instance, in a historic first, and one of the most recent assertions of this, in 2019, the Tokyo Metropolitan Government introduced a specific Nightlife Tourism Promotion Subsidy to encourage greater night-time activity, with up to 100 million yen available for each grant., As a story that is certainly commonplace in many of our cases throughout the book, the Japan Tourism Agency, which has been particularly proactive in advocating for this night-time activity, has unsurprisingly been looking closely at London's evolution of night-time activities so as to experiment in Japanese megacities with similar approaches, albeit perhaps more cautiously, if not timidly.

A matter for wards?

As in London or Amsterdam, and indeed just like in Manchester, the case for greater attention to the night-time in Tokyo is certainly more and more clearly articulated and has now found an official voice not only in the capital, but also across the country, via the founding of the Japan Nighttime Economy

Association (JNEA) in 2019, which is now emerging as a proactive voice in the night-time governance conversation. Yet, before these developments took place, much of the initiative came from 'below', both in the private sector and in governmental terms. Up to the time of writing (December 2020), Tokyo has had no official night-time strategic planning (or vision) document or night mayor/manager at the metropolitan level – represented in the Japanese capital by the Tokyo Metropolitan Government and its governor. To a degree, the intention to improve Tokyo's nights exists in several official documents, especially, as noted earlier, when it comes to economic growth and tourism, but it also remains dispersed in a variety of policies and vision-setting agendas, none of which really puts specific emphasis on the night. In this relative government vacuum, business groups have been the drivers of the current round of discussions about night matters, with transportation taking a prime spot in this more informally driven metropolitan debate. However, the direction of this emphasis has perhaps gone away from the models of London or New York. Emerging from the 24-hour transportation debates and even a pilot programme in 2013 targeting night-time worker mobility, transport has been a relatively attentive area of night-time engagement. Yet, it has also been driving in the opposite sense to London and New York, in that it has progressively seen a focus in proposals moving, as much of the rest of the debate, towards tourism needs instead of local commuting and night-shift workers.

Where the night-time governance conversation has perhaps been particularly proactive, then, is at the more localized level of wards and neighbourhoods. In a city of over 13.6 million people, with a metropolitan government authority covering just over 13,000 km², it is at the local level that most night-time innovations have been happening in Tokyo. As one of Japan's 47 prefectures, Japanese law designates Tokyo as a *to* (都 ['metropolis']), managed by a metropolitan government overseeing 23 municipalities or *tokubetsu-ku* (特別区 ['special wards']), along with 26 *-shi* (市 ['cities']), five *-chō* or *machi* (町 ['towns']), and eight *-son* or *-mura* (村 ['villages']), each of which has a local government. At local municipal level, several of the special wards with rich nightlife and tourism resources have been particularly proactive in spearheading night-time programmes. Therefore, for instance, while Shibuya has had an official night guide for tourism, Toshima has been developing more explicit strategies to manage how evening cultural activities can be used to benefit late-night entertainment, hospitality and clubbing. Of course, these 'lower-level' municipal practices are important in feeding night-time thinking and development to the Tokyo metropolitan level, but this degree of localized, ward-driven innovation has thus far not scaled upwards to the regional government or, indeed, the national one, but rather inspired to some degree private initiatives like the JNEA.

Two exceptions to this are the issues of public transportation and licensing. All public transportation has thus far been managed more directly at the metropolitan level in the name of efficiency, while, to date, licensing policy, which is made at the national level, has left little flexibility for wards. Yet, aside from some moderate consideration of after-hours issues in these two areas of metropolitan action, night-time thinking remains outside the concerns of Tokyo's major governance structure. Alongside wards, business, as in other cases seen here, has also taken to 'the streets' in the absence of more centralized decision-making. However, this consideration should not immediately lead us to think of purely privately run models like that of Amsterdam. Even in this relatively private sphere, national political matters are central in determining the direction of night-time politics. For example, the city's Night Time Economy Association – perhaps the most significant organization targeting night economy development over the last few years until the launch of the JNEA – was, in fact, started by the current ruling party (the Liberal Democratic Party). Compared with the active level of night-time discussions of this association, there is instead no noticeable reaction or counter-initiative from opposition parties like the Party of Hope, which is led by current Governor of Tokyo Koike Yuriko. Yet, this already flags up how national political matters easily insinuate themselves into even the seemingly private orientation of business managers. What this tells us, then, is that party politics here might make it harder for Tokyo to translate national-level proposals into a comprehensive metropolitan-level strategic plan for the night economy, and that, in any case, national political considerations become important drivers even of a business-led reality like that of Tokyo's night-time governance.

Nonetheless, pilot programmes and experiments are still commonplace at the municipal ward level, many of them with close public–private partnership bases. Among them, perhaps the most famous one, and a clear predecessor to the JNEA, comes from the ward of Shibuya. This ward appointed a night ambassador linked to its Shibuya Tourism Agency as a symbolic figure to testify to, and speak for, the ward's intention to develop Tokyo's NTE at an internationally visible level. The current ambassador, Zeebra, is a famous rapper who has been particularly active in advocating for the clubbing industry and has contributed to the recent relaxing of the 'no dance' law that has affected the development of Tokyo's after-hours entertainment. With some parallel to Amsterdam, Zeebra's duties involve promoting Shibuya's nightlife to local consumers and tourists while overseeing and lobbying for a better NTE at different governance scales, in particular, at the metropolitan level. This has led, for instance, to the development in 2018 of a 24-Hour Tokyo Promotion Committee, aimed at initiating pilot night-time projects at the city level with the hope to consolidate cross-ward and overall metropolitan night-time planning and policy in the years to come. Again, beyond the ward level and the emerging private-sector-oriented JNEA, much of the current activity remains driven by the Japan Tourism Agency. For instance, in 2019, it launched a programme to support 13 model night-time 'businesses', such as the Aoyama night-time farmers market, in order to showcase the variety of night venues and to encourage a wider reading by both local businesses and tourists of the night-time offer, centred not just on the Japanese capital, but across the country.

Unsurprisingly, as the COVID-19 crisis hit Japan's NTE, not least through the eventual postponing of the much-anticipated 2020 Tokyo Olympic games, much of this conversation quickly pivoted towards recovery. One of the official governmental reactions was to launch a Council of Revitalization of Nighttime Tourism Resources (with JNEA representation), a Japanese tourism agency focused on nightlife, though again only from this relatively narrow perspective. More broadly, and again outside the domain of national or metropolitan government, the JNEA has been relatively proactive at providing resources, information and advice for night-time operators on how to adhere to COVID-19-related regulations and access support in dire times for night-time-oriented industries.

24-hour Berlin: night-time governance from the grass roots

Much of the recent international drive for night-time advocacy has gone, virtually or physically, through the heart of Germany. Berlin's NTE is a regular reference point for cities around the world. It is popularly characterized, perhaps in somewhat of a counterpoint to Tokyo, by its liberalism. It has been tagged as an 'anything-goes' approach, where visitors and residents alike can find whatever they desire at all hours of the night (Colomb, 2013) – at least before the COVID-19 crisis. Local businesses and night advocates have leveraged this tag. This image has been marketed throughout Berlin's 365/24 campaign, for instance, which has touted the 'diversity' and 'creativity' of Berlin at all hours. The 365/24 campaign has been stressing the range of night-time possibilities, from the mainstream to the particular, and from the 'high' culture of classical music to specific niche cultures of night-time entertainment, going through the well-established name the city has in techno and rock music.

While the city is particularly well known for its vibrant and innovative creative arts scene, Berlin's world-renowned music scene is perhaps the largest economic drawcard. Characterized by much-chronicled 'hot spots' like the

Berghain nightclub and an array of music venues, ranging from small jazz bars to large, informal warehouse parties (Neate, 2014), the diverse and innovative nature of Berlin's music scene has attracted the global likes of MTV and SoundCloud, as well as weekend 'techno-tourists' from across Europe made possible by cheap airfares (Garcia, 2018. For a long time, Berlin's vibrant nightlife, along with low rents and other favourable dwelling conditions, has been a drive for other cultural industries to the city. Put simply, the city is perhaps one of the best examples of the agglomeration power of the NTE industries in driving varied audiences to a place (Merkel, 2012).

Just like in Tokyo, Berlin's vibrant nightlife and creative arts scene have been shaped significantly by the city's history as a war-torn city. Berlin suffered considerable upheaval and destruction throughout the Second World War, and its development trajectory was splintered by the division of the city. Following the fall of the Berlin Wall, the uneven economic, social and political geographies that manifested during the Cold War period remained important markers shaping the trajectory of urban economic development in a more and more 'global' city. These conditions drew creative communities to East Berlin that quickly developed an array of artistic studios, squatter settlements, nightclubs, bars and live music venues (Sheridan, 2007). These communities, often closely connected to specific nightlife venues, continue to have a lasting impact on Berlin and its ongoing relationship with the night. Yet, as in London and, to a degree, Tokyo, many community spaces centred around night-time venues have been progressively displaced by, or 'integrated' within, Berlin's growing visitor and transnational economy. Many of Berlin's most famous and successful nightclubs, for example, started out in these informal spaces whereas some artistic communes have prolonged their survival through government subsidies, as well as by eventually needing to appeal to the growing 'tourist dollar' (Jones, 2018. It is in the wake of this growingly tense context between internationalization for the visitor class and unsteady positioning of communities that rely on the night-time that Berlin has also developed bottom-up urban night-time governance mechanisms. These have emerged predominantly from the private and community sector, and have focused on ensuring that the city maintains its cultural and nightlife vibrancy beyond profit-driven rationales. Chief among these, at least in terms of international notoriety, is the Club Commission. Yet, before we jump into this repeatedly cited example, we should highlight the contrast in interpreting and facilitating the NTE that Berlin presents to Tokyo.

Berlin has a long and proud history as a supporter and promoter of both creative industries and the NTE. Arguably, Berlin is a pioneer of the 24-hour city, with all-hour venue and liquor licences available in the city from as early as 1949 (Bader and Scharenberg, 2010). Berlin's constitution even contains the obligation 'to preserve and promote a liberal artistic life' (State of Berlin, 2018). This history of artistic and night-life liberalism continues to this day, with Berlin's NTE enjoying an enviable regulatory environment (Bader and Scharenberg, 2010). Berlin's largely hands-off approach has allowed a large variety of different subcultural night-time venues to emerge and flourish. In addition, these venues are supported by an abundance of all-night food and alcohol outlets and 24-hour public transport services, all made possible through a supportive governance environment. Private sector consultancy (and chief voice in this space) Creative Footprint highlights that Berlin's music industry enjoys strong access to 24-hour licences, funding opportunities and authorities and politicians via advocacy groups. This narrative contrasts strongly with cities such as Sydney and London, which have seen their rich diversity of venues replaced with 'profit-driven, upscale/corporate forms of nightlife' (Hae, 2012) due partly to cumbersome regulation and lack of political voice.

This is not to say that Berlin's NTE is without challenges. In several ways, Berlin has been the victim of its own success, with a steady increase in contestation over its NTE since the beginning of the 21st century (Füller et al, 2018). Berlin's strong attraction as a destination for firms and individuals has seen its flourishing nightlife become entangled in processes of gentrification and concerns regarding the coexistence of the NTE with growing residential populations (Füller et al, 2018). In response to this growing contestation, NTE groups decided to collectively represent their interests by forming the Berlin Club Commission in 2001 (Sisson, 2016). The commission acts as the 'network for Berlin's club culture', through its leadership from Lutz Leichsenring, spokesperson for the commission and a major voice in the international NTE debate, who has become an integral and powerful voice for Berlin's NTE and, to some degree, been acting as Berlin's informal night mayor. It undertakes a large variety of tasks, ranging from acting on behalf of venues in city planning issues and gathering and disseminating research, to assisting venues with admin, soundproofing and operational matters. It has also enjoyed constant dialogue across Berlin's two-tier system of government, and its proactive approach sees night-time issues rarely dealt with through the reactive and, at least according to some, damaging government interventions that characterize other cities throughout the world. The commission's work has led to the incorporation of a music venue map into the Berlin planning system, which now requires developers to consult with venues before new projects are commenced, and the raising of funds and lobbying for subsidized rents for artists. The challenge has become ever-more live recently year as the COVID-19 crisis hit the city.

Local politics matters: awakening the Historic Quarter of Valparaiso

Situated only 120 km from Santiago, Valparaiso was a major merchant port on the Pacific coast of South America in the 1800s and a popular stop for travellers on their way to the California Gold Rush. However, the golden years of Valparaiso came to an end with the opening of the Panama Canal in 1914, an event that marked the beginning of a slowdown in the city's development and its transition from a port city to a smaller tourist destination.

Setting up a nocturnal 'delegate'

Two events made 2003 an important year for Valparaiso. In May, the Chilean Senate officially recognized the city as the country's cultural capital, and a few months later, the United Nations Educational, Scientific and Cultural Organization (UNESCO) designated its historic district as a World Heritage Site. Once known as the 'Jewel of the Pacific', Valparaiso was considered a testimony to early phases of globalization and an excellent example of late 19th-century urban and architectural development in Latin America. With a natural amphitheatre setting that inspired many artists and poets like Pablo Neruda, the city's early industrial infrastructure and monumental architecture wonderfully inhabit its challenging topography of steep hills accessible only through stairways and its distinctive funicular elevators.

This designation was initially seen as an opportunity to develop the city and to strengthen its image as a cultural and tourism destination around the world. However, it could not stop the slowdown and decline that was already under way, particularly in the city's seaport district or Barrio Puerto, which has lost most of its residents and becomes a ghost town after dark. This situation is made worse by a large student population that, in the absence of affordable nightlife activities, gathers in empty stairways and plazas to drink and socialize at night, making noise, urinating and disturbing neighbours wishing to sleep.

Following the lead of Amsterdam and other cities that have appointed night mayors and nocturnal governance structures, in 2017, Mayor Jorge Sharp designated a Delegado Nocturno ('nocturnal delegate') responsible for promoting collaboration among residents and the nightlife industry, and reactivating the city's night scene in a safe and productive way. One of the main responsibilities assigned to this role was to help regularize night-time practices in public and private spaces by mapping the distribution and impact of licensed venues, and working with the police to identify illegal businesses. These activities were seen as key tasks in recovering the city's legacy as a World Heritage Site and its reputation as a safe tourist destination.

Local politics strikes back

The person selected for the role was a former businessperson and club owner, Juan Carlos Gonzalez. One of Gonzalez's contributions was to help create the Asociación de Locatarios Nocturnos de Valparaíso ('Nightlife Business Association of Valparaiso' [ALNOVAL]). Created in 2018, the goal of this organization was to promote greater collaboration between local hospitality businesses and the city in order to better regulate the sector's practices and elevate its reputation. ALNOVAL helped organize important local events, such as Valparaiso's 2018 New Year's celebration, which gathered thousands of tourists at the Barrio Puerto. However, residents and local authorities reported several incidents and irregularities during the festivities, such as their culmination more than one hour past the time they had been authorized. A study conducted in 2018 and 2019 revealed that rather than seen as an advocate or champion of citywide concerns for its night scene, the nocturnal delegate was perceived as a 'lobbyist' or promoter of the interests of the nightlife industry. Several council members and representatives of local groups criticized the lack of transparency of his administration and the absence of a 'master plan' with clear goals and expected results. Following corruption charges and allegations that he was 'leasing' liquor licences, the nocturnal delegate resigned in November 2018 and Mayor Jorge Sharp announced the creation of a Citizen Safety Division, which will allow the municipality 'to better handle the issues in Valparaiso's night scene' (Seijas, 2020a). While the nocturnal delegate role no longer exists in Valparaíso, it finally placed the night on to the city's agenda, recognizing its rich nightlife history and the need to reactivate its Historic Quarter after dark.

Comparative insight: the evolution of night-time governance in Bogota

While nuisance can happen anytime throughout the day, sensitivity to the impacts of night-time activity – particularly entertainment – increases significantly after dark. Throughout this book, we have encountered many examples of restrictive policies that regiment or restrict the use of time in the hope that this will help reduce externalities such as noise, crime and antisocial behaviour. Among them, the Cabaret Law in New York and the lockout laws in Sydney are instances of tough police enforcement to manage urban areas after dark. In Latin America, the most prominent of these measures comes from Colombia.

In 1995, when Bogota had one of the highest crime rates in the world, then Mayor Antanas Mockus established a regulation known as *Ley Zanahoria*

('Carrot Law'). This policy banned nightlife and alcohol sales after 1 am in order to prevent accidents and violence in the Colombian capital. A study by Universidad de Los Andres revealed that only 8 per cent of the reduction in the number of homicides in Bogota between 1995 and 1999 can be considered an effect of this law. However, even in the absence of empirical studies that proved the advantages of this measure, this law became a regional model of citizen security and the first account of a 'temporal dimension of violence' (Dammert Guardia, 2007). Many other Colombian cities, such Cali and Manizales, as well as other Latin American capitals like Panama and Asunción, implemented their own versions of the Carrot Law throughout the 1900s and early 2000s.

Just as tensions between regulators and the police led to the emergence of sub-economies in Tokyo, this zero-tolerance approach to night-time alcohol consumption also led to the rise of a large underground – and mostly illegal – night scene in Colombian cities. Additionally, restraining the operation of nightlife venues in central urban areas encouraged the emergence of other venues in peripheral neighbourhoods located outside of the law's jurisdiction, such as the world-famous Andrés Carne de Res, a large restaurant and nightclub located 45-minutes away from the centre of Bogota. In the absence of public transportation or taxis to reach these remote destinations, many patrons were involved in alcohol-related accidents on their way to and from these establishments. In response to this issue, Andrés Carne de Res introduced the 'route angel', a service that quickly became a staple of Colombian nightlife culture. 'Route angels' are responsible drinking programmes by which patrons can hire a designated driver from a third party – often private taxi companies or ride-hailing services such as Uber – that can safely drive them home after a long night of partying. These innovative practices not only helped diversify night-time mobility options in a large city that has very limited night-time public transportation, but also paved the way for a more proactive approach towards managing the city at night.

In the early 2000s, private sector entities such as Asobares – Colombia's Bar Association – began to raise awareness of the need to build strong alliances among nightlife business owners and with local authorities in order to change the often negative perception of the sector. Since 2014, Asobares has organized 'Expobar', an annual forum that gathers together the most prominent representatives of the nightlife industry in the country to discuss common challenges and opportunities. With support from the city council, in 2015, Asobares led the creation of *Sello Seguro* ('Safe Seal'), a recognition provided to licensed establishments that achieve high security and quality standards in their services. The Safe Seal allows these businesses to stay open for two additional hours on Thursdays, Fridays, Saturdays and the days preceding national holidays. It also provides them with institutional support, which enhances their reputation with both patrons and residents. Among the requirements, businesses that wish to obtain the Safe Seal should: have evacuation plans and hold evacuation drills once a year; have fire protection kits and emergency exit alarms; have trained security personnel and a designated driver scheme; and encourage patrons to be respectful towards neighbours when leaving their premises.

In the following years, a series of local policies illustrated a renovated and more enabling approach towards the city's NTE. In 2016, Bogota's Security Secretariat and Corpovisionarios launched *Farra en la Buena* ('Responsible Partying'), a citizen culture strategy that promoted safe and non-violent ways to experience nightlife in Bogota. In 2017, the Office of the Mayor of Bogota launched a project to revitalize the *Zona Rosa*, a highly commercial district with one of the highest nightlife densities in the city (118 bars and nightlife venues, several casinos, and nine hotels). The goal of this project was to recover public space and enhance safety, mobility, cleanliness and lighting in the area. In 2018, Bogota's city council approved Agreement 706, a regulation that supported a '24-Hours' strategy that could extend trading hours for retail and services to promote greater productivity in the city, and created the possibility of establishing a Night Management Office to oversee the implementation of this strategy in Bogota. That same year, Bogota's Economic Development Secretariat commissioned an exhaustive study to guide the strategy, while the city's Culture Secretariat, Art Institute and Chamber of Commerce hosted 'Nocturnal Cities', the first Latin American 'Conference on Managing the City at Night'. This event, co-curated by Sound Diplomacy and Andreina Seijas, gathered more than 20 international experts and advocates in Bogota to discuss common challenges and analyse the relevance of the growing role of night mayors for the region (Seijas, 2019).

In the context of the COVID-19 pandemic, creating a night-time governance strategy for the city has gained new prominence and momentum. In December 2020, the Economic Development Secretariat organized a pilot exercise in the Chapinero commercial neighbourhood as a strategy to support the reactivation of the sector, which has been gravely affected by the pandemic. This ten-day pilot allowed restaurants, nightlife, culture and leisure businesses to stay open for one or two additional hours, and led to a 35 per cent increase in sales in the area. Based on its success, the city plans to organize other pilots to further test the advantages of incorporating more flexible trading hours to help businesses bounce back from the current crisis. The Safe Seal programme has also provided a useful platform for businesses to rebuild trust with patrons and local authorities, as businesses that have the accreditation are more prepared to handle crowds safely and efficiently implement social-distancing regulations.

6

What Night-Time Agendas?

Introduction

With urban politics come urban interests and agendas – even at night-time. To acknowledge this even more explicitly than in Chapters 4 and 5, this chapter discusses common themes and strategies described throughout the various cases in the book, with an emphasis on what commonplace issues have driven NTE action. It journeys across NTE strategies, sound and crowd-management methods, safety and crime schemes, and transport and logistics solutions to depict what key themes emerge in the night-time governance of cities, as well as what is left out. Importantly, it also offers a specific view on the issue of urban equality at night-time, and the emerging vulnerabilities that scholarship, and some practice, have been highlighting – from homelessness to night-shift workers, marginalized neighbourhoods and segmented mobility. Moving along with the narrative of Chapters 2 to 5, the key concern of this chapter is to broaden the reader's imagination of what the NTE is. Here, we focus on what is being governed in cities after hours, from a relatively restrictive view of the NTE as a fulcrum for entertainment and hospitality, to including the likes of transport, logistics and healthcare, and going further to recognizing those voices and activities that are often silenced by night-time discussions. Critically, we underscore here the importance of strategic visions and strategic plans in consolidating what night-time agendas are at play in cities.

What kind of 'night' is it?

The night-time has become an increasingly popular realm of policy and action in many cities around the planet. Yet, what is there to be managed at night in cities? In previous chapters, we investigated the ways in which cities around the world have been testing and building night-time governance institutions. What agendas underpin these approaches? In this chapter, we aim to discuss the common themes and strategic orientations that local governments have been taking when it comes to managing their urban life 'after dark'. Night-time planners and managers have cast a relatively broad eye at what is to be at the heart of night-time agendas. Several cities have continued a well-established tradition of NTE thinking that, as we discussed in Chapter 1, has provided much of the thrust beyond the popularity of night-time governance. Others have been venturing into questions of sound and crowd management, as well as safety provision and crime-prevention schemes (Crawford & Flint, 2009). Some have moved into regulating transport and night-time logistics solutions, to name but some of the issues at stake. However, there are, of course, several more agendas at play here. Obviously, with the advent of the COVID-19 pandemic, many of these issues have either been heightened, as with sprawling concerns about the challenging recovery of night-time hospitality and entertainment, or indeed skewed, as with issues of transport, safety and, indeed, inclusion.

These moves underline how night-time agendas are emerging as commonplace in the governance of cities at night. Yet, at the same time, this underscores the need to better unpack what, and who, is left out from current night-time management practices the world over. These 'silent' agendas are an equally essential element of the governance puzzle that we paint here and very much an issue animating the rest of the book. As we began to do in Chapters 1 and 2, here, we stress again the need to broaden our imagination of what the NTE is, and what is to be governed in cities in the after hours. We outline lessons emerging from what has already been put in place, as well as areas that, to date, remain out of the spotlight in many cases, perhaps as a result of a commonly restrictive view on the NTE as a fulcrum of entertainment and hospitality. Importantly, foreshadowing a more explicit attention to urban equality that we present in Chapter 7, we call for night-time management to include the 'production' side of the NTE, not just the 'consumption' of its core offers. This implies attending to those workers and services that, for instance, uphold transport, logistics and healthcare as the backbone of how cities function at night, as well as during the day, beyond what has made it into the headlines of media and planning documents to date. In turn, this consideration speaks volumes to the fact that, in many cases, much of the work that goes on at night-time is essential in keeping cities ticking as 24/7 realities in need of continual attention, maintenance and support.

Night-time agendas are, of course, still very much a part of a nascent field of both strategic practice and inquiry. Notably, despite the proliferation of night-time councils, commissions and offices in local governments the world over, there is currently only a small portion of cities that showcase dedicated night-time strategies and vision documents. As we have seen, cities like

Paris, Amsterdam and London have been said to lead the way in terms of creating explicit manifestos and visions for their respective NTEs. Likewise, contexts like Sydney and Geneva also testify to the inclusion of nocturnal elements and considerations into recent municipal discussion papers and strategic urban plans. However, we should not forget that as much as they represent a positive international trajectory in the recognition of night-time governance practices, these moves remain limited to a degree in numbers and experience, and most cities globally still lag behind on this front. To a certain extent, the expansion in explicit night-time strategies is also the result of these cities' night-time offices and authorities having limited legislative and planning powers, with many cities left chiefly to promote dialogue and discussion between key stakeholders. In this sense, these strategies have come in as visions to make key recommendations regarding the future of night-time services, amenities and policies with their residents, industry partners and visitors' best interests at heart, rather than issuing actual policy and implementing it. Equally, many 'night-time' issues require coordination efforts beyond city limits. For instance, in many cases, interventions related to night-time workers' rights and fair pay still fall within the remit of national or state governments and also require the involvement of employers across a range of sectors, who might not be used to working with city governments. The paucity of tangible and explicit policy actions regarding night-time agendas has enabled further dependency in many cities on third sector and partner organizations in galvanizing the discussion regarding the night-time offering that cities have, as is the case in Zurich and Berlin. Many night-time services and policy interventions have been outsourced to third sector organizations across the Global North and South. Overall, then, we are confronted with a patchy landscape of evidence from which we can draw systematically but that still speaks to the emerging complexity of managing the urban night. We will return to this strategic planning issue at the end of the chapter after more in-depth consideration of the sectors that, to some degree, remain on the margins of the night-time governance discussion. Luckily, despite the lack of bespoke nocturnal policy, there is a wealth of pledges and 'soft' initiatives being undertaken and supported by city governments around the world that we draw on to some extent here. These might be identifiable within four main key thematic areas: that of the NTE (more or less narrowly understood); that of noise management; that which brings into question safety and crime; and that which pertains to night-time transport and logistics. In spite of the relative infancy of explicit 'nocturnal thinking' at the city level, these four main strands have a number of shared variables, and some issues and solutions can be seen to overlap. In the following, we begin by summarizing these, then move on to the issue of what is perhaps still out of the commonplace picture and conclude by casting an eye onto the challenges and blind spots of night-time strategy making.

Focusing on the NTE

As we detailed in previous chapters, there is a well-established tradition of NTE research and, to quite some degree, practice. Yet, this tends to be confined specifically to an urban economy that is predominantly synonymous with the entertainment and hospitality sectors. Undoubtedly, this agenda has been the key driver behind initial discussions regarding the management of NTEs in many cities. It has involved a focus on the regulation, licensing and practices of night-time businesses, mainly represented by nightclubs, bars and other leisure and hospitality venues. In many cases, these have been engaged, or, indeed, have also self-organized, in more or less loose coalitions of operators, such as liquor licensee forums in contexts like Manchester and Melbourne.

The creation of resources and information targeted specifically towards venue managers and those entering the NTE business sector is an approach favoured by North American cities, with San Francisco, for instance, creating a web-based handbook for business owners in 2016 that outlines permits, licensing, zoning issues and strategies for dealing with the management of noise at night. Similarly, in 2017, Pittsburgh's NTE manager developed a work plan that outlines the creation of a resource for improving NTE business compliance (Harnden, 2017). New York City followed suit in 2018 through a collaborative project with the NYPD and the New York City Hospitality Alliance, creating a 'best practices' guide for nightlife establishments, with emphasis on security measures. From this perspective, the limits placed on night-time offices and managers in relation to policymaking and legislation also lead to an approach in which research and engagement with citizens and stakeholders enables recommendations to be made to local authorities that have the power to influence planning and policy. The Greater London Authority utilized this approach in its 2017 'Culture and the night time economy: supplementary planning guidance' (GLA, 2017b), outlining recommendations to borough councils around protecting pubs by granting them status as an asset of community value. These recommendations do not directly create policy, but rather encourage local authorities to act upon aspects of the London Plan in tandem with utilizing the UK's National Planning and Policy Framework as a tool to combat the decline in venues. This is, of course, a prime area for further policy development post-2020, considering the economic shock created by pandemic lockdown responses – an issue we will revisit in Chapter 8 dedicated to COVID-19 recovery.

Yet, as we illustrated in Chapters 4 and 5, this overall focus has also been put in place by 'authorities' other than local government. Early European night-time governance initiatives, such as in Berlin, Zurich and Amsterdam, demonstrate the approach through which independent third-party organizations, external to city hall, can lobby for the interests of NTE businesses and provide a platform for dialogue between policymakers and stakeholders. In the case of Amsterdam's Night Mayor Office (detailed in Chapter 5), being an independent foundation allows for this NTE agenda approach to centre its work predominantly on protecting the interests of the nightlife sector in the city. In doing so, it has worked with local government to introduce 24-hour licences to a number of venues in the city, an initiative that is seen to not only boost the economy, but also diversify the geography of nightlife venues in the city (Koren, 2018) and to alleviate congestion in the small hours, as partygoers filter home over a longer period of time than usual (Baer, 2016).

To be certain, this agenda has not just been limited to economic strategies; rather, the importance of the arts and cultural sector in the urban night also require involving actors in the field of cultural policy in night-time planning. From a cultural perspective, the safeguarding of well-established venues has enabled cities to build a reputation for the provision of particular cultural offerings (music, theatre, opera, visual arts and so on) and, in several cases, has been seen as crucial to the promotion of nightlife for the purposes of tourism and leisure. Yet, for the most part, the focus on the NTE in major cities like London, Sydney or New York originally centred on making an economic case for the value of the night-time. As we saw in previous chapters, this has taken the shape of statements by both local authorities and, perhaps even more commonly, business leadership organizations like London First, which have advocated for the sizeable financial output of night-time activities and the width of employment underpinning many of the core economic sectors operating in cities when the lights go down.

In turn, for municipal governments and local council officials, this agenda tends to surface important tensions in the management of the night-time. The intersection between maintaining existing cultural offerings at night, ensuring residential areas are not adversely affected by nightlife in the city and the providing infrastructure and services is broadly illustrated by three different approaches of cities. First, some have focused on the provision of licensing, security and permit information for NTE business owners, typically defined as night-time business 'operators'. This has predominantly focused on compliance purposes, centred on regulation and licence issues that, as seen in the vast diversity of governance models in cities around the planet, has remained particularly contextual to local and national conditions.

Second, night-time-oriented recommendations made by night-time offices, managers and coalitions of various sorts for the consideration of local authorities have been directed towards (but often not explicitly part of) local government planning and policymaking. Third, other approaches have focused on the mediation, facilitation of dialogue and, in some cases, conflict management between NTE establishments and policymakers whose policy orientation has not always been seen favourably by NTE operators, even in the many cities that we have outlined as conversant in night-time management.

Tackling night-time noise, safety and crime

A prominent realm of action for night-time policymaking is certainly that of safety and security, with a wide variety of examples available out there; in many cases, this sector of local action is the main, if not only, proactive one in night-time thinking. The intersection between crime and policing agendas leads to numerous appraisals and options when tackling safety in the night-time city. With limited direct powers, the most prominent and successful city initiatives have involved mediation between existing third parties, along with outreach and engagement with citizens to alter behaviour and foster particular zones of nocturnal activity. Much has emerged over the last few years as regards protecting groups and spaces that might be perceived as vulnerable and objects of particular risks 'after dark'. The theme of gender at night has been central in London and Nantes in particular. For example, London's Night Czar Amy Lamé recently established a Women's Safety at Night Summit and Charter (in 2017). In addition, the city of Nantes has discussed gender and public space workshops with key stakeholders as a means to engage citizens and proprietors with issues around safety and gender. Other key initiatives seen as successful and shared as best practice between cities that have been proactive in night-time planning involve the employment of volunteer groups in prominent public spaces, such as red-jacketed 'square hosts' in Amsterdam's Rembrandtplein (in 2018). These hosts act as on-the-ground soft enforcement and surveillance teams, and encourage a convivial atmosphere. Moreover, since 2013, Melbourne City Council has worked directly with the Salvation Army to provide 'street teams' that foster a positive attitude among partygoers and have proven to reduce crime in inner-city areas. Melbourne, in particular, puts an emphasis on safety, and its own official strategy most closely aligned with nocturnal priorities is the 'Beyond safe city strategy' (Melbourne, 2014a), most recently updated in 2014, but with limited explicit mention of the night-time.

Similarly, a key topic in discussions regarding the night in many cities is that of noise. Mitigating noise is a concern that not only appears in debate regarding venues in urban centres and their relationship with neighbouring residential developments and projects, but can also be seen to be prominent in discussions concerning the behaviour of citizens and groups in urban space. In this regard, in 2016 and 2017, some cities, such as Nantes and Orlando, worked to create 'night stations' to concentrate nocturnal gatherings in public space, with emphasis on revellers and late-night patrons when exiting establishments and on mitigating the risks of disturbing the surrounding environment while waiting for transport. Primarily, though, the mitigation of noise can be traced to early agendas concerned with managing the tensions between urban regeneration and residential development, and the safeguarding of key music and entertainment venues in cities. As has been noted, this issue can be seen as a catalyst for the rise in NTE management discussion in the 21st century.

Enabling the continuing provision of entertainment in venues throughout the night with the least disturbances to surrounding developments has been problematic for many cities, with clear evidence provided that many licensed venues have closed in recent years as a result of noise complaints and disagreements with residents in neighbouring developments (Roberts, 2018). To tackle this issue, a key policy principle has been championed across numerous cities, which places emphasis on those responsible for new developments to ensure that noise mitigation is embedded within their design and provisions from an early stage through to completion. The so-called 'agent of change' principle and its equivalents provide an example of cross-cutting policy that enables cities to recommend or implement planning approaches to managing nocturnal urban space and the needs of multiple stakeholders with minimal opposition. Prominent examples include Melbourne (statewide in Victoria as of 2014), San Francisco (in 2015) and London (in 2018). Once again, this strand of night-time action underscores the continuing importance of the private sector and consultancy in pushing the conversation about after-hours planning and policymaking. A recent publication from the music consultancy organization Sound Diplomacy has highlighted a number of strategies in South America that involve place-making and revitalization initiatives to encourage varied demographic groups to enjoy the night through festivals and events in contexts like Bogota in Colombia, Rosario in Argentina and Asunción in Paraguay. These initiatives require the cooperation of numerous actors and public creative and cultural agencies but have proven successful in regard to the overall inclusivity and positive perception of the night, all without dedicated night-time offices overseeing the operations but rather through cooperation between existing departments.

Planning for night-time transport and logistics

As part of the 24-hour-city agenda, many cities are reviewing and debating the adequacy and expansion of night-time public transport provision. Transport plays an integral role in facilitating activity at night and is perhaps one other area of policymaking that stands out as commonplace when it comes to experiences of night-time planning and governance. Some metropolitan authorities and local governments embracing night-time agendas have extensive powers over transport planning in their locality, explaining why transport has been an increasingly popular area of intervention for night-time planning. A legible, available and well-maintained public transport network is required to meet the needs of workers, tourists and residents alike, and night-time provisions have long been available in many cities. Increasingly, as cities expand and as nocturnal activity zones diversify and proliferate across urban centres and beyond, the need for the reappraisal and extension of existing transport is becoming apparent. This is reflected in the activities of numerous cities within this study, often accompanied by a (re)branding of particular transport services in order to emphasize their nocturnality. Paris and London, for instance, have long had extended services of night buses running, but cities are increasingly expanding their transport offers with measures explicitly targeting night-time consumers. The weekend 'Night Tube' in London is a prominent recent example, as is the 'Firefly' service in Nantes, both of which provide explicit reference to the night in their titles. In London, night-time interventions focusing on transport have sought to provide transport infrastructure to facilitate the movement of people to support the functioning and growth of the NTE (McArthur et al, 2019). As previously discussed, some cities identified within this report, such as Orlando and Nantes, have recognized the need to manage the clusters and zones in urban centres where people congregate at night, often waiting for taxis and other forms of transport after exiting nightclubs, bars and other venues. The requirement of good planning in this regard is twofold because it must consider not only transport provision issues, as well as congestion on both roads and pavements in the city, but also the impact of sound on local residents and businesses. Existing research has shown that, in general, these policies tend to focus on addressing consumers' needs and fail to acknowledge how different groups of people move and experience the city at night (Hadfield, 2014; Talbot, 2016; Plyushteva, 2019; Smeds et al, 2020), a point we discuss in more depth in Chapter 7.

Less discussed among city planning guidance or vision documentation is the potential for easing congestion during the day through the rescheduling of deliveries of goods and services in the city. This has been explored to some extent by the cities of San Francisco and Portland, and was discussed by former London Mayor Boris Johnson in 2013. At this juncture, though, the implementation of such schemes appears to be difficult to execute, as such services often involve multiple stakeholders and partners from the public, private and sometimes third sectors.

Planning for night-time workers?

While several agendas have been creeping (differentially, depending on context) to the forefront of night-time planning, the people behind the actualization of those agendas tend to remain 'in the shadows'. In fact, much of the industry of the NTE remains clearly out of the spotlight: as we have been arguing thus far throughout the book, there remains a clear consumption bias when discussing and planning for the night-time. Critically, the role of night-time workers tends to be sidelined in favour of the consumers of night-time activities, chiefly in the entertainment and hospitality sectors, with limited attention for those that service these areas, as well as the likely much wider group of maintenance, public order, healthcare and logistics workers who have their livelihoods centrally dependent on night shifts and night-time employment. For example, few and limited policy initiatives in the many cities we have already flagged are focused on questions of the well-being, working conditions and practices of the maintenance workers who are often essential to keeping our cities ticking over by adjusting their infrastructure, ensuring safety and attending to the cleaning and 'resetting' of workspaces, as well as areas of mobility and consumption, from offices and shopping malls, to kerbsides and pavements.

A well-cited 2011 report from the London-based Young Foundation, titled *Rough Nights* for example, exposed the growing dangers of working at night that hundreds of thousands of workers faced. More recently, in France, a 2016 report published by the National Agency for Food, Environment and Work Health and Safety concluded that night-time workers: suffer from systemic lack of sleep; are more subject to risks of cancer, diabetes, obesity and hypertension, to name only a few; and are more exposed to conflicts with other groups of people active at night. The Young Foundation report also exposed the diversity of contexts for night-time work, ranging from the commonplace night shifts (roughly between 6 pm and 6 am), to more complex realities like the so-called 'continental shift' (with rotating employment in sets of mornings, afternoon or nights in different days), three-shift working (with weeks of nights followed by weeks of days) and ad hoc occasional arrangements that change as needed. In London, the Royal College of Nursing reported on the large number of healthcare professionals working twilight shifts, usually finishing work around 1–2 am (Smeds et al, 2020). Improved legislation, better evidence and awareness of night-shift working, and more appropriate support structures all stood out as pivotal to protecting a clear sector of the workforce that, as the Young Foundation noted, tends to be out of the scope of much policymaking, suffering directly from the already-poor coverage that night-time issues and economies confront across the board (see also Robin and Charpentier, 2019). Central in this depiction is a call for nuance in understanding how night-time workers operate and what their conditions might be, even despite now-plentiful medical evidence pointing to clear impacts of night-time working on circadian rhythms and stress, heart and degenerative conditions, and, indeed, more generally, the well-being of the millions that work in cities after dark the world over. In turn, paying closer attention to the workers and 'producers' of the NTE also surfaces issues of migration and diversity in the workforce that, as we will detail in more depth in Chapter 7, are essential for authorities and night-time advocates to attend to.

From night-time agendas to night-time strategies

The evidence we have sketched thus far speaks to a variety of agendas that have been emerging in cities around the world when it comes to shaping activities that take place after dark. The role of the NTE, albeit restrictively and typically with a bias towards the hospitality industry, has certainly taken off in many contexts. Noise, safety and crime issues also stand out as well-established themes of night-time governance that play long-standing roles in debates in many cities in the Global North and South. Transport and logistics – perhaps not as centrally as either safety or the economy, but still with growing appreciation – have also been commonplace sectors for some of the night-time initiatives that we have recounted thus far. Far less commonly, these agendas have paid limited to no attention to the workers who underpin much of these sectors, an issue that we will unpack more extensively in Chapter 7. Yet, as a whole, the three dimensions of economy, safety and transport begin to paint an initial picture of the kind of mixed agendas that night-time governance can span – not including the issues of recovery from and responding to the COVID-19 crisis, which we will also unpack in Chapter 8. Yet, many of these agendas have often lacked an important element of governance: that of strategy.

Night-time strategy making is very limited and poorly institutionalized. While it is present in some shape (but rarely is there a standardized way to do night-time strategy), in most contexts that have already set up a night-time governance responsibility via a night mayor, night manager or similar role, the mechanisms to generate sound after-hours planning are still either embryonic, sector-specific or altogether non-existent. At the same time, strategic approaches to night-time planning are mostly lacking at national or regional levels, with also few metropolitan-scale initiatives, highlighting the pressing need for a whole-of-government understanding of what happens after hours. As illustrated in Chapters 1 and 2, the movement towards night-time governance remains predominantly driven by some municipal governments, business coalitions and, in some cases, community and advocacy groups. As we have highlighted, much of the conversation and policymaking is typically driven by private sector alliances and organizations who tend to represent the major 'interests' of the night time. This is not necessarily a negative factor per se, but it stresses the continuing ad hoc nature of how night-time agendas are corralled in cities around the planet and discussed by stakeholders in urban governance. From that perspective, there are limited cases of consultative and engagement processes, such as the night czar's 'night surgeries' in London, which are capable of feeding directly into night-time policymaking and planning. In turn, this has clear implications as to whose agendas and what particular interests are represented in night-time governance structures, plans and interventions. In turn, apart from a few cases that we have underlined already, night-time governance the world over is confronted by a dearth of institutionalized consultation systems, not least participatory planning and community input mechanisms. Finally, and as importantly, we would argue, these systems rarely present a sound institutionalization of a specific night-time-oriented evidence base or, indeed, established paths for the mobilization of specific night-time expertise in local government, which is often relegated to the advice of consultants, academics and advocacy coalitions. While these actors have certainly been important in driving greater and greater attention for the night-time in cities around the planet, and while, of course, we have been participants in these lines of more or less informal advice ourselves, the call to institutionalize night-time strategy making and its underlying governance processes certainly spurs a concurrent need to ensure that sound information about night-time conditions is available to policymakers.

7

Whose Night is It?

Introduction

Inequality is one of the most defining features of the 'urban age' (Gleeson, 2014): crucibles of opportunities and socialisation, cities are equally at the heart of today's greatest social disparities (McGranahan & Satterthwaite, 2014). The urban night is far from immune to these challenges, and potentially a key space for engaging questions of equity, participation and inclusion. In this chapter, we explore issues of what we could call 'invisibilization'[1] (Vergès, 2019) in current approaches to night-time governance. Specifically, we argue that the ways in which NTEs are framed, discussed, defined, delimited and understood in policy conversations tend to obscure the intersecting racial, gender-based and socio-economic inequalities that shape and, indeed, maintain 'thriving' NTEs (and urban economies more broadly).

Reframing 'the economy' in NTEs

Cleaners, carers and nurses, drivers, logistics and factory workers, security agents, and sex workers, to name only a few, have been a foundational part of formal and informal NTEs for a long time. In addition, the 24/7 running of (urban) capitalist economies is enabled by the gendered division of work (Katz, 2001), with women undertaking the main share of the social reproduction tasks of cleaning and caring at home and at work during the day, late in the evening, throughout the night and early in the morning. As already argued elsewhere, whether concerned with equality or not, the work of government policy always involves the discursive construction of subjects to be governed (Smeds et al, 2020). This, in turn, shapes whose voices are included, excluded, taken into account or discarded in decision-making. In this chapter, it is our contention that the contribution and lived experiences of those who make cities run after dark, through paid and unpaid, formal and informal work, remain all too often invisible, and thus neglected, in mainstream visions of the urban night. Therefore, in asking 'Whose night is it?', we wish to draw attention to how enduring inequalities and injustices shape the ways in which different bodies can safely work, or just be, in the night-time city.

Throughout this chapter, we explore whose experiences remain largely absent from policy conversations about and dominant visions of NTEs. It is our hope that by making these omissions visible, a more nuanced view of NTEs can emerge, one that: recognizes that the development of urban NTEs de facto generates and supports the reproduction of economic, social, racial and gender-based forms of injustices; stresses the need to cater for the needs of those who are the most vulnerable at night, whether because of their economic status, the nature of their job, where they live or their gender, age, race or physical ability; and recognizes that 'the economy', as a statistical category and sector for policy intervention, does not fully account for the range of nocturnal activities that contribute to the (re)production of our urban societies, lives and, indeed, economies. Therefore, with this in mind, the next sections first draw attention to the hidden inequalities of the domestic, formal economic and public spheres after dark. We then expand our argument on the need to shift attention to workers (instead of consumers) in urban NTE governance. Finally, we argue that urban policy actors have a key role to play in reframing 'the economy' in NTEs around values of care, solidarity and inclusion. Before we delve into these issues, it is important to stress that this chapter draws in large part on insights from two studies of night-time inequalities in London: one focusing on transport provision for night-time workers carried out by two co-authors of this book (Smeds et al, 2020); the other one looking at nurses' experiences of working night shifts in the British capital (Kabala and Robin, 2020).

Injustice and the urban night

In popular discourses and imaginaries, the NTE evokes theatres, restaurants, bars, concerts and entertainment after dark. It is true that for some, the city after dark is synonymous with endless opportunities to celebrate and enjoy nightlife. Often, these enjoyments are made possible by the low-paid and precarious work of waiters, bar tenders, cooks and performers. Research has shown that not everybody is equal when it comes to enjoying the city after dark, with sexual, gender, income and/or racially motivated forms of exclusion still shaping who can or cannot access nightlife venues and public spaces after dark (Roberts, 2006; Schwanen et al, 2012; van Liempt et al, 2015 Talbot, 2007).

For many, often women, the city after dark is synonymous with a second (unpaid) work shift: caring for relatives at home after a full day of work in the city. The London nurses we met for our research all recounted the exhaustion that results from working night shifts and caring for kids and relatives at home during the day. For another large group of people, often people of colour, the city after dark means a long commute from home to a cleaning, logistics or security job in a fancy, inner-city office tower or a hospital, or to warehouses and factories. For others, again often women and people of colour, the night means heightened exposure to the risks of gender-based, racially motivated and/or sexual violence, as well as police harassment. Some people, if given the choice, would never leave their homes after dark because the city becomes uneasy and unsafe to navigate, particularly if these people are old or live with any kind of disability. After dark, there might be fewer people to help you, fewer transportation services running and fewer station staff to ask for help or information. To be clear, these kinds of inequalities are not all specific to the night, nor are they restricted to cities. Racial and gender-based discrimination and uneven exposure to male and police violence, as well as ageism and disability-based exclusions, are pervasive and systemic features of many hetero-patriarchal, ageist, racist and neo-colonial societies. These issues have been made impossible to ignore by the global Me Too movement and Black Lives Matter protests, to name only those. Some have shown that these kinds of discriminations and injustices are not only pervasive, but also necessary to the reproduction of capitalist economies (Katz, 2001; Vergès, 2019). However, these injustices continue to exist and take specific forms after dark, and they tend to be concentrated in cities. While many people have the privilege of enjoying the comfort and safety of their homes at night, it is important to remember that large groups of often low-paid night workers have to navigate the city at a time of reduced public transport frequency, and with fewer people and spaces to keep them safe and interact with them. What is perhaps most obvious, and somehow counterintuitive, to any astute observer, nocturnal bus rider or city wanderer is that a lot of these invisible lives become visible at night, if one takes the time to look. How is this accounted for in current planning around the NTE?

A focus on night-time transport planning offers an interesting case to explore some of these issues because workers' and consumers' capacity to move safely, and in an environmentally sustainable way, across the city at night is essential to building inclusive and sustainable NTEs. This requires supporting access to affordable, reliable and low-carbon public transport. Research has shown how transport access is unavoidably linked to inequalities and broader questions of social justice. Pereira and colleagues (2017: 183) have argued that transport justice can only be achieved if interventions 'prioritise vulnerable groups', for instance, elderly, disabled, minority ethnic and low-income groups. Mimi Sheller (2018: 48) deploys the concept of mobility justice as 'an overarching concept for thinking about how power and inequality inform the governance and control of movement'. In doing so, she focuses 'attention on the politics of unequal capabilities for movement, as well as on unequal rights to stay or to dwell in a place' (Sheller, 2018: 26). Sheller's work invites us to recognize that we do not inhabit the same bodies, and that our bodily experiences of moving across the city during the day and throughout the night are shaped by a range of individual characteristics and broader social, cultural and economic forms of discrimination.

While night-time studies is still an emerging field, existing research has shown that urban night-time policies generally fail to consider the differentiated experiences and needs of different groups of people moving across cities at night (Hadfield, 2014; Talbot, 2004; Plyushteva, 2019). Studies have explored how different groups' perception of the safety of night-time transport shape their decisions to travel. For instance, Oviedo Hernandez and Titheridge (2016) demonstrate how perceived lack of safety leads low-income groups to avoid public transport at night. Others have shown how gender-based inequalities play out in these processes, highlighting similar fear-based transport exclusions for women (Yavuz and Welch, 2010; Abenoza et al, 2018). These are particularly important issues to consider when thinking about NTE planning – even beyond transportation – because whether people can freely and safely move in the city at night shapes workers' experiences and urban dwellers' willingness and capacity to go out at night and enjoy the city. In that sense, public realm interventions focusing on lighting, architectural design and landscaping to enhance feelings of safety and togetherness should be important elements of NTE planning, alongside the provision of adequate, reliable, safe and affordable transport options, particularly for workers.

In our own work on London's night-time transport planning (Smeds et al, 2020), we observed that women feel particularly unsafe riding in minicabs and Ubers for fear of being subject to sexual violence. In response to these issues, the Greater London Authority produced a Women's Night Safety Charter and a broader Violence Against Women and Girls Strategy. Such efforts are welcome and show the need to recognize how individual characteristics (in this case, gender) shape whether and how one can navigate the city at night. However, our research also showed that night-time policy discourses and strategies in London still fail to fully grapple with the 'politics of difference' (Young, 2011 [1990]) and how this shapes who the night-time city is for. With a focus on the mobilization of specific forms of representation in London's night-time planning policy, our research revealed 'how techniques of government shape whose mobility (at night) is valued, rendered explicit and governable, but also whose mobility is rendered invisible in dominant policy discourses' (Smeds et al, 2020: 4). Our analysis found that, overall,

London's night-time policy discourses tended to universalize 'nocturnal mobile subjects' and displayed very limited recognition of differentiated mobility needs. Specifically, policy documents tended to highlight the needs of universalized consumers (encompassing visitors, Londoners and young people) to a larger degree than those of workers. London's night-time policy documents do acknowledge that workers' mobility tends to be more difficult and less smooth than that of consumers. They also recognize that without night-time workers, the city would stop functioning. Yet, night-time transport policies such as the Night Tube focus on the safety and ease of travel of consumers to and from night-time consumption hotspots and only run on weekends, neglecting the needs of the large flock of night-time workers working throughout the week (McArthur et al, 2019). Of course, these types of policies also cater for workers working in the entertainment and nightlife industries. Yet, they do not address the needs of workers employed in hospitals, office buildings, logistics or maintenance work who need to travel to other places of work that are located far from nightlife hotspots. What changes to the design of transport infrastructure, streets and public spaces would be undertaken if night-time mobility policy took the differentiated needs of urban dwellers seriously? It would require exploring what moving at night would mean for immigrant women, sex workers, wheelchair users, the elderly, young black, Asian and minority ethnic men, nurses working night shifts, exhausted warehouse workers, and many more.

Asking 'Whose night is it?' also requires looking more closely at the types of 'night-time cultures' that are excluded from dominant NTE discourses. Research has shown that structural forms of discrimination and broader dynamics of gentrification shape what kinds of 'nightlife cultures' are deemed desirable in the NTE. Talbot and Böse (2007) explored how the criminalization of black youth and black culture led to the de facto exclusion of black cultural venues from NTE strategies in Manchester and London. The authors argue that this exclusion is further reinforced by urban regeneration strategies and gentrification dynamics, discriminating licensing practices, and racially motivated policing. Their work clearly stresses the need for greater attention to racial exclusion in the night time economy (Talbot 2007) and to how systemic forms of discrimination (as perpetrated, for instance, by the police) continue stigmatizing particular kinds of cultures and venues. Campkin and Marshall (2018; also see 2017) published a landmark report on the large-scale closure of LGBTQI+ venues in London, driven primarily by gentrification. In this specific case, the report was particularly influential in shaping policy discourses on the need to preserve London's LGBTQI+ spaces, yet it remains difficult for decision-makers to find ways to address these issues through night-time planning. These works highlight the inherent tensions and contradictions brought about by NTE agendas as a continuation of growth-oriented urban development policies. Without questioning the fundamentals of these strategies, and without designing planning and fiscal interventions that address the risks of gentrification (for example, rent control, protecting culturally significant businesses and shops, and so on), night-time agendas are likely to continue exacerbating the inequalities brought about by neoliberal urban developments. This is also likely to contribute to the erasure of cultures and venues that have played a key role in creating a thriving and vibrant urban nightlife in the first place, particularly for historically marginalized and discriminated against groups. Asking 'Whose night is it?' requires us to attend to these issues.

Putting night-time workers into the spotlight

Originally, the NTE concept was used to describe economic activities in the arts, entertainment and hospitality sectors, particularly in cities in the Global North (Bianchini, 1995; Shaw, 2010). In this context, governing the urban night was also seen as an opportunity to trigger economic growth in inner-city areas by expanding leisure and consumption activities later through the night (Talbot, 2007). With policy discourses and strategies centred on designing attractive night spaces for consumers, workers' needs have received comparatively less attention. Observers have long shown the invisibility of workers in the maintenance, care, logistics and security sectors, as well as sex workers, in dominant representations of NTEs (for example, MacQuarie, 2017b). In London, for instance, a report by the consultancy Ernst & Young (2016) shows that night-time workers are more likely to work in the transport and storage, health and social care, and administrative sectors. Arts, entertainment and recreation only account for 6.4 per cent of the workforce, and hospitality (hotels, restaurants and bars) only for 13.4 per cent (McArthur et al, 2019). As already mentioned, our research showed how London's night-time strategies focused on consumers and did not address workers' needs. This means, for instance, that night-time workers have very limited travel options available. They have to rely on off-peak transportation services – characterized by lower frequencies and greater chances of scheduled engineering works. Night buses are currently the only public transport mode available between 1 am and 5 am during the week, with 51 per cent of passengers using this service to travel to or from work, according to TfL estimates. The London Royal College of Nursing indicated that healthcare workers finishing shifts between 12 am and 2 am have less travel options, have to wait longer for buses and face longer journeys, often involving multiple changes.

In the opening section of her recent article, entitled 'Capitalocene, waste, race, and gender', feminist and decolonial scholar Françoise Vergès (2019) eloquently describes the process of invisibilization of racialized women working in the early hours of the morning and late hours of the night. This section is worth quoting at length:

> Every day, in every urban centre of the world, thousands of black and brown women, invisible, are 'opening' the city. They clean the spaces necessary for neo-patriarchy, and neoliberal and finance capitalism to function. They are doing dangerous work: they inhale toxic chemical products and push or carry heavy loads. They have usually travelled long hours in the early morning or late at night, and their work is underpaid and considered to be unskilled. They are usually in their forties or fifties. A second group, which shares with the first an intersection of class, race, and gender, go to middle class homes to cook, clean, and take care of children and the elderly, so that those who employ them can go to work in the places that the former group of women have cleaned. Meanwhile, in the same early hours of the morning, in the same big metropoles of the world, we can see women and men running through the streets, rushing to the nearest gym or yoga center. They follow the mandate to maintain healthy and clean bodies of late capitalism; they usually follow their run or workout with a shower, an avocado toast, and a detox drink before heading to their clean offices. Meanwhile, women of color try to find a seat for their exhausted bodies as they return on public transit from cleaning those gyms, banks, insurance offices, newspaper offices, investment companies, or restaurants and preparing meeting rooms for business breakfasts. They doze off as soon as they sit, their fatigue visible to those who care to see it. The working body that is made visible is the concern of an ever growing industry dedicated to the cleanliness and healthiness of body and mind, the better to serve racial capitalism. The other working body is made invisible even though it performs a necessary function for the first: to clean spaces in which the 'clean' ones circulate, work, eat, sleep, have sex, and perform parenting. But the cleaners' invisibility is required and naturalized.... Women who clean, whether they live in Maputo, Rio de Janeiro, Riyadh, Kuala Lumpur, Rabat, or Paris, speak of the very little time they sleep (three to four hours), of the long hours devoted to their commutes, and of the work they have to do once they return home. Women who perform caring/cleaning jobs all talk about being exhausted.

As already mentioned, the nurses who gave us their time to discuss the challenges of working night shifts all stressed the exhaustion that comes with caring for patients and their families throughout the night, dealing with aggressive behaviours in the hospital, and going back home to take care of their families (Kabala and Robin, 2020). MacQuarie (2017a) has explored the health and social impacts of night shifts on migrant workers in London, such as physical exhaustion, isolation and lack of access to modes of collective representation. In turn, this limits their ability to advocate for a greater recognition of their rights and experiences in night-time planning strategies. COVID-19 has revealed the importance of key workers in the health and care sectors, as well as in logistics, transportation and maintenance. Key workers continued working day and night while the majority of us stayed at home, protecting ourselves from a possibly deadly contamination. Those in low-paid jobs who did not own a personal car kept using public transport in the middle of the pandemic.

Night-time strategies are a tremendous opportunity to build cities that are more sustainable, for instance, reducing congestion by moving some transport, retail and logistics activities to the night-time. However, if more people are to work at night, then the needs of low-paid, night-time workers have to be better understood and accounted for within these strategies. It is not just about offering night-time workers decent pay and affordable and safe travel options. Decision-makers and urban night managers also have to face important ethical questions: do we really need to expand NTEs? What kinds of NTE is desirable for a society that seeks to be more just and environmentally sustainable? Is it necessary to promote NTEs that are fuelled by warehouse developments and relentless online shopping, creating precarious and low-paid jobs to triage, transport and distribute ever-expanding numbers of goods, 24/7, across the city? What are the consequences on the health and well-being of workers, and on the carbon footprint of cities? Given the stark inequalities and climate emergency that our urban societies face, particularly in the so-called 'Western world', these are not trivial questions. All too often, night-time agendas have not just encouraged the consumption of services that contribute to thriving urban life (for example, culture, arts, entertainment, food and so on), but also supported the relentless consumption of useless, polluting material goods around the clock, with dire consequences for the planet and the low-paid workers who constitute the living infrastructure that enables excess consumerism.

Progressive night-time policies are possible. Paris, for instance, has introduced a set of experimental interventions to improve night-time cleaners' working conditions (in 2010). This includes revising public office cleaners' schedules so that they can work during the day instead of the night. It was shown that making cleaners visible and part of the 'daytime' workforce not only improved working conditions, but also allowed cleaners to feel that their work is more valued and respected by building users. This example shows that it is possible for decision-makers and night-time managers to stop and ask themselves what type of activities can be moved to regular day shifts. It will be necessary to continue health, care and some forms of maintenance and logistics work around the clock. In these cases, designing adequate, accessible and safe outdoor and indoor spaces, supporting those on low-paid jobs, and improving night-time transport offers could help improve night-time working conditions. This includes, for instance, introducing a standard living wage that reflects living costs in cities where housing and transport prices are high, reduced fares on public transport, and improved public transportation services throughout the night. Other promising initiatives have emerged to better cater for night-time workers. In Sweden, for instance, 24-hour childcare services are available to parents working at night. In Nantes (France), the civil society organization Paloma, which offers legal, social and healthcare support to sex workers (often migrant women and men), has been involved in the municipality's Night Council initiatives to map out different groups' vulnerabilities at night. Through these initiatives, Paloma acted as a boundary organization to help sex workers engage with the night-time strategy of the city of Nantes. As representatives of Paloma noted: 'it was the first time an institution took the time to meet with them and ask for their opinion'.[2] Sex workers were asked to comment on: their needs at night (for example, food, sleep, safety and healthcare concerns); how a night-shift working schedule impacted their access to healthcare and housing; and the forms of interactions (conflicts, solidarity and indifference) they experienced with other people using urban spaces at night. As part of this consultation, several citizen-led recommendations were formulated to inform the Night Council's strategy. These are promising initiatives that can inspire inclusive night-time planning going forward.

Towards inclusive night-time planning

Our contention in this chapter is that urban managers and policymakers interested in the night need to grapple with the 'politics of difference' (Young, 2011 [1990]) in order to design strategies that can support justice-oriented night-time planning and the emergence of inclusive NTEs. As reiterated throughout this chapter, differences in ethnicity, gender, disability, age, religion and economic status can be done and undone through particular policy interventions (as exemplified, for instance, in the case of London's transport policy). Asking 'Whose night is it?' requires us to address uncomfortable issues of invisibilization, exclusion and injustices. It requires us to ask what forms of injustices are obscured in dominant representations of NTEs, and how are they (re)produced or challenged through particular policy interventions. It demands us to attend to both issues of representation and policy action to make visible and cater for those who make our cities run after dark, whether in the 'formal', nationally accounted economy, in the domestic sphere or in so-called 'informal' or 'illegal' economies. It requires attention to those who are excluded from public and private night-time urban spaces. It also demands deeper reflections on the impact of 'daytime' policies on vulnerabilities at night: in London (and the UK more broadly), the closure of homeless, women and migrants shelters as a result of austerity measures means that homelessness is on the rise, migrants cannot get access to legal aid, health and housing support, and many women who attempt to escape situations of domestic violence might end up on the streets. At night, these populations are more vulnerable to abuse, whether from other people or from the police. Inclusive night-time strategies should, therefore, look beyond 'nocturnal' interventions to also consider how daytime policies (for example, social care policies and the availability of shelters in cities) address vulnerabilities that are heightened through the night.

Asking 'Whose night is it?' also requires us to reckon with another equally uncomfortable question: *what is the night for?* What is the pertinence of the NTE agenda if it only contributes to support activities that create exploitative, low-paid, precarious and exhausting jobs that are predominantly taken up by groups that already suffer social and economic disadvantages (for example, women, migrants and people of colour)? The COVID-19 crisis has made visible the range of key workers that sustain our economies and lives. It has also revealed the deep inequalities entrenched in our consumerist societies. While the most privileged could shield in their homes, access a wealth of goods through online shopping and stream the latest Netflix series from their sofas, others were exposing themselves to the virus, delivering clothes, pizza, bottles of wine and electronic goods for low salaries, and for lack of a better choice. One-day deliveries of predominantly useless goods are enabled by an invisible, yet very much real, infrastructural system linking consumers to online shops, to warehouses, to logistics workers and to deliverers, all of whom work around the clock. Nurses, carers and doctors were getting ill saving the lives of others throughout the day and throughout the night, commuting to and from work, by car if they had the choice, by public transport if they had no other option. Obviously, these issues cannot be addressed solely by urban managers and will require multi-level governance. However, recognizing how night-time strategies can enhance pre-existing injustices, or, on the contrary, how they can challenge them, is necessary. The practical and ideological orientation and related exclusions of urban night-time policy and planning frames, tools and practices should not be overlooked, for they are a product of (and contribute to reproduce) broader injustices and uneven power relations.

Notes

[1] We began expanding on this invisibilization issue and on the need to recognize the contributions of nurses, drivers and maintenance workers in Robin et al (2017); we reiterate this in other forms in Acuto (2019) and Seijas (2020b), overall stressing that the visibility of the producers, not just the consumers, of the night time economy is essential to this NTE agenda.

[2] Translated from French by the author. For more information, see: www.ch-le-vinatier.fr/ orspere-samdarra/rhizome/anciens-numeros/rhizome-n77-reveler-la-nuit-juillet-2020/ reduire-les-risques-la-nuit-avec-les-personnes-travailleuses-du-sexe-2740.html

8

The Night-Time and the Pandemic

Introduction

The global crisis ushered in by the COVID-19 pandemic in early 2020 hit cities the world over hard. Even harder hit, through lockdowns and stretched essential services, has been the world of the NTE and management. Yet, at the same time, the movement to institutionalize and discuss and campaign for the night in cities (depicted in previous chapters) also laid some important ground for tackling this, and NTE movements are already afoot. Drawing from media reports, current research, events and direct experiences by the authors, this chapter analyses how these night-time governance structures have responded to COVID-19 and shares some insights into how this crisis might reshape the way night scenes are managed around the world. The goal of the chapter is to contextualize the 'primer' introduction of the previous sections in the wake of one of the deepest disruptions of our century: what will the NTE look like in the future? What can be learnt and leveraged from the way COVID-19 unfolded after dark? What will happen to the trends, themes and institutions that flourished up until 2019 in a world radically challenged by the health, and economic, crisis of COVID-19? Our goal in this chapter, then, is to underline how the crisis has been impacting the trajectories and realities discussed thus far, seeking to look ahead at how these might change or return to the fore, rather than simply drawing conclusions as to the outcomes of COVID-19 when the global crisis that emerged from the pandemic is still, almost certainly, under way.

Deepening night-time challenges?

It would be hard to conceive of a practitioner-oriented primer for urban governance without accounting for the deep disruptions ushered in by 2020 in cities the world over. Undoubtedly, the impact of the COVID-19 crisis has been staggering for urban development. From our point of view, this is especially so when we consider its bearing on the NTE and its associated industries. It might still be too early to tell what the full extent of the COVID-19 disruptions is on NTEs more specifically, or nightlife more in general, but as many night advocates and policymakers from the cities chronicled in this book have already underscored, the crisis might have set much of the advancements detailed in previous chapters back by years. Due to the lockdowns, social-distancing measures, health and well-being impacts, and socio-economic and political impacts characterizing the last 12 months, much is now at stake globally when it comes to managing, and recovering, nightlife in cities. Importantly, we think that the COVID-19 crisis offers an apt window into the challenges, and possibilities, for urban governance 'after dark'. The pandemic is a particularly poignant time of reflection to understand how we can rethink our governance relationship with nightlife in cities. What already seems clear at the time of writing (between November 2020 and May 2021) is that the crisis has underscored, perhaps once again, the fundamental social and economic function of the NTE and of nightlife in cities.

The arts, culture and entertainment have been in the eye of the storm of the pandemic. Downturns, lockdowns and shifts in socio-economic conditions around the planet all but shut down the vast majority of the 'core' NTE business in most cities, while fundamentally disrupting wider night-time industries like maintenance and logistics, and clearly putting 'on the line' healthcare, as well as service and delivery, workers. Hence, the urban night's COVID-19 crisis has extended quite clearly to those industries and workers, like cleaners, drivers and nurses, who have often been even more in the shadow than their entertainment and hospitality colleagues. The externalities of disruptions to major daytime activities have also been severe in most cities. Logistics workers that, for instance, service major trade and retail stores have been at the joint risk of losing their jobs and performing them in even more challenging conditions for health and well-being throughout the crisis. Critically, COVID-19 has underscored how the people in those jobs that support nightlife and the NTEs of cities have been at risk, and quite often in dismal circumstances, around the planet. While we do not want to sketch a chapter that easily summarizes such a complex crisis, especially due to the diversity of conditions between the cities described in this book, there is already little doubt that this is a reality that is likely to be felt by NTEs and workers for many years to come. Hence, we think that the crisis has, to some degree, heightened some of the deepest troubles that nightlife has been facing in recent years across major cities as much as more regional and smaller realities.

This is the case, for instance, of the impact of COVID-19 on homelessness in major cities. The crisis has been a driver not only of further displacement, but also of further insecurity for those sleeping rough as health services became increasingly overwhelmed in major cities around the planet. If it is already quite clear how the burden of disease is already tipped against those in vulnerable and precarious conditions, like the homeless population, these have become even starker in the wake of COVID-19. This, in turn, has seen many essential night-time support services like shelters and kitchens struggling to meet mounting and complex demands, while both confronting financial, social-distancing and other new-found pressures. Examples of engagements to provide rapid responses to this situation include, for example, the city of Toronto's CA$6.1 million funding package to shelters and 24-hour respite sites, including the provision of PPE and wage increases for shelter workers pushed into increasingly demanding shifts. Yet, the leadership of major cities has also fast been criticized for its limited engagement with the questions of homelessness as the COVID-19 crisis expanded. This is the case, for instance, of New York City, where Mayor Bill de Blasio was subject to sizeable complaints and advocacy in favour of better measures for the homeless population throughout most of the first months of 2020, which was eventually resolved when the city turned to providing shelter to thousands of rough sleepers in empty hotel rooms in April 2020. Relocation to unused hospitality venues like hotels and motels has been a common trend internationally. For instance, Greater Manchester had already moved to dedicate a £5 million package to accommodate hundreds of homeless people in hotel rooms across the city-region. This went hand in hand with an emergency £100,000 to the homelessness charitable sector, along with an appeal calling on local big business and wealthy individuals to donate funds to support voluntary, community and social enterprises during the COVID-19 crisis. However, more widely, this has been coupled with growing concerns around the capacity to provide adequate testing, medical support and health (or crisis) information to the many facing homelessness on the streets of increasingly locked-down and policed cities. Examples like Manchester, Toronto, New York and many, many others are encouraging and, in the long run, could possibly usher in greater attention for night-time challenges such as homelessness support when it comes to the management of social justice after hours in cities. Yet, throughout the crisis, homelessness advocacy organizations and research centres have highlighted how we might be headed towards even harsher conditions emerging from the lack of shelter, as COVID-19 pushes many more who were confronting really precarious socio-economic situations into conditions of homelessness.

COVID-19 has also further highlighted the precariousness, fragility and lack of recognition that many night-time workers and industries face, and had already been confronting for quite some time, as regards the well-documented well-being risks of night shifts, with often unhealthy and poorly remunerated working conditions, which could further worsen in the years ahead. The crisis has shed light on the millions of essential workers that keep our economies running 24/7 and provide vital care to those of us who need it. They have enabled many of us to stay at home while keeping a semi-normal life (we are speaking from London, Melbourne and Boston). The crisis has revealed that those who work around the clock have no alternative but to keep working during a pandemic, often for low wages. It has also shed light on other enduring metaphorical and real pandemics: that of violence against women, with domestic abuse figures skyrocketing in many countries; and that of housing precarity, with homelessness figures dramatically increasing and many people being forced to stay inside in poor accommodation with increased risks of exposure to the virus. The crisis has also revealed the deep inequalities that make up the NTE of our cities today, with many informal and marginalized workers around the world having to choose between economic survival and their health. This has, for instance, been the case of sex workers.

The year 2020 saw repeated calls made by human rights groups such as Amnesty International to include sex workers much more clearly in the COVID-19 response. As in the case of many other vulnerable groups, sex workers have been confronted by conditions of exclusion from social and economic support schemes launched in the wake of the crisis. The impact of COVID-19 also meant that they faced an increased difficulty in accessing essential health services. This has not only been in relation to COVID-19 screening and support, but also gone hand-in-hand with sex workers confronting health systems that were progressively unable to attend to critical matters such as HIV treatment and other forms of critical health support for the industry. As the crisis began to overwhelm any such systems in cities around the planet, it also heightened the degree of criminalization of sex work and the securitized response of many authorities to sex workers in the wake of calls for greater social distancing and lockdowns. While a large part of sex work provided in person has declined or disappeared altogether, this has had a clear and tangible impact on the lives and livelihoods of these workers, many of whom are tightly intertwined with NTEs. It has also prompted increasingly pressing demands for shelter, as well as further issues such as mental health problems, drug addictions and even more basic needs such as access to food and education. Prominent academic and community advocacy in the likes of the *Lancet* or by organizations like the Sex Workers Rights Advocacy Network have stressed that there is now a pressing need not only for emergency measures and greater recognition within the realms of vulnerable workers extremely affected by the circumstances of the crisis, but also for the leveraging of the current context for the production of social and legal reforms. COVID-19, once again, drives us towards the need for greater attention to questions of discrimination and marginalization that have been exacerbated by the crisis. This not only applies to sex workers; it also points to the impact of the crisis on many other vulnerable segments of the night-time workforce like carers, as well as many cleaners, small night-time traders and drivers, without even beginning to account for the millions working in the so-called 'informal economy', which we flag up in the following.

The crisis has also heightened the fragility of the tenure of many NTE businesses and initiatives in an already-complex and, in some cases, hostile market across many cities, as highlighted by, for instance, Alessio Kolioulis (2020), drawing on the work of Ben Campkin and Lo Marshall at University College London. The crisis has further stressed the impact of land-use pressures and the problematic lack of institutional recognition and institutional safety nets for many of these businesses. This is especially true when it comes to those who cater to vulnerable groups or who provide for those who have an already-heightened sensibility to urban development and speculation. At the same time, consumer spending and capacity to leverage funding to keep businesses (and workers) afloat has been dramatically diminished. This has gone hand in hand with the very tangible physical inability to keep night businesses, community activities and many other forms of urban nightlife open.

COVID-19 has, in turn, had an even more devastating impact on the livelihoods, and, in many cases, pre-existing fragility, of the informal economy, including its specific night-time components. For instance, the International Labour Organization (ILO) of the UN has highlighted how the crisis quickly affected informal enterprises, with consequences such as the immediate loss of revenue for most informal economic units and workers, likely leading to an even greater surge in urban poverty in many urban areas around the planet. Yet, perhaps paradoxically, the crisis has also witnessed an expansion in the informal economy because of the collapse of the more formal system and many micro, small and medium-sized enterprises unable to cope with the burden of COVID-19. From this perspective, then, not only have informal livelihoods been fundamentally put at risk by the crisis, but COVID-19 might have also heightened the difficulty with which many of these workers and enterprises operate. This has likely presented greater risk of contagion and even less capacity for overcommitted support systems to provide additional help.

In turn, for the most part, informal workers have remained outside of many countries' existing social protection schemes and forms of relief and economic assistance for the crisis, with informal night workers struggling to access respite and recovery packages or grants. At the same time, it is also important to underscore how informality has, in many cases, been the realm where vulnerable groups (at times ostracized by the formal mechanisms of urban governance) have been able to access support and response mechanisms to confront the crisis. From this point of view, an important issue that pertains to the informal dimension of the NTE is how the COVID-19 crisis and its response provide key opportunities to build greater and more effective partnerships with institutions that play this role for night-time workers and night-time livelihoods. While several have emerged during the crisis, many others have a long-lived history of operation in providing engagement, support and a voice for informal workers. This engagement, in turn, could allow many cities to shift from policing and forced moves towards formality, to a greater recognition of the operation of a sector than, in many urban areas, especially in developing countries, accounts for a sizeable percentage of the population and the workforce.

The 24-hour city, interrupted

Social activity and interaction are an essential part of urban life, particularly life at night. Severe travel restrictions and social-distancing measures have created many challenges for nightlife, tourism and the festival industry, as they rely heavily on socialization. Shutdowns, curfews and so-called 'Cinderella Laws' have been adopted by cities all over the world to prevent the propagation of the disease, but their restrictive nature also affects the nocturnal ecosystem: night-time jobs disappear, supply chains are broken and habits, particularly social ones, eventually change. These dramatic changes have two main impacts. On the one hand, they demand more flexibility from a regulatory standpoint. In some places, they have paved the way for exceptions that allow businesses, artists and other nocturnal actors to operate more freely in what is known to be a highly regulated policy space. For instance, since March 2020, the state of New York allowed restaurants, bars and taverns to sell alcoholic beverages off-premises through pickup or delivery as long as they were sold with food (New York State Liquor Authority, 2020). This created a lifeline for many businesses that pivoted to in-house dining and cocktails as a way to survive amid the crisis.

On the other hand, these changes created incentives to develop more local and decentralized night scenes. As covered in Chapter 2, nightlife and entertainment uses have traditionally been situated through licensing and zoning laws in specialized districts, separated from residential uses. As more people work from home, and as public transit options become more limited to travel to and from city centres at night, CBDs might gain new residents while peripheral neighbourhoods might witness a renaissance of their cultural and entertainment offers. Decentralizing amenities such as nightlife, leisure centres and creative spaces could help create medium-intensity entertainment hubs rather than congested areas where tensions between residents and revellers tend to be exacerbated. Additionally, in line with the '15-minute city' concept promoted by cities like Paris, a hyper-local urban agenda could help reduce the carbon footprint of the music industry while promoting local talent and stimulating more diverse local NTEs.

This redistribution of entertainment uses can be actively encouraged by local governments introducing mechanisms such as the 24-hour permits system in Amsterdam, which incentivizes small businesses and entrepreneurs to set up shop in peripheral city areas by providing more flexible trading hours and regulations. By incorporating these mechanisms, cities could achieve not only a spatial redistribution of entertainment uses, but also a more temporally diverse night scene, with staggered rather than monolithic trading hours that facilitate crowd management and mobility. In line with these objectives, in July 2020, Amsterdam announced that it was granting six new 24-hour licences, increasing the total number of businesses holding these special permits from nine to 15 (Stichting Nachtburgemeeser Amsterdam, 2020). According to the Night Mayor Foundation, these new permits will allow more businesses to recover from the crisis, as some clubs are already providing different functions, such as listening sessions or renting out their spaces in the morning for yoga and other activities.

Urban systems of night-time governance were historically formed based on the claim that night-time activity is a nuisance that must be remediated. Over the past 30 years, new institutions have emerged based on a celebratory concept: the night is an area of opportunity. These contrasting perspectives have led to two types of nocturnal policies: on the one hand, restrictive policies such as curfews and dancing bans; on the other, enabling policies such as 24-hour licensing schemes. While some cities favour either a restrictive or an enabling tradition, many fluctuate between the two. As history demonstrates, following a crisis or a dramatic night-time event, such as a violent death or a terrorist attack, night-time regulations flip from one extreme to the other like a pendulum. In this context, power shifts back from nocturnal networks to the police, particularly in highly polarized environments. Examples such as Sydney's lockout laws illustrate how vibrant nocturnal environments can suffer from restrictive measures implemented as a reaction to violence and crime. This 'pendulum effect' becomes even greater in times of crisis (Seijas, 2020b). This can be seen in city responses to contain the COVID-19 crisis, most of which involve curfews. Rather than reactive responses, this calls for data-driven decision-making in the context of shocks and emergencies that will continue to shape night-time governance in the future. For a start, the pandemic will make it difficult to ignore that the NTE is much broader than nightlife and entertainment, since even without restaurants, entertainment and hospitality businesses closing during nationwide lockdowns, a large group of night-time workers kept our cities afloat, facing high risks. This, in turn, calls for more inclusive night-time strategies that explicitly focus, first and foremost, on the needs of workers, as discussed in Chapter 7.

9

Urban Governance after Dark: Eight Propositions

Introduction

What does one need to know about managing cities at night? And, what is the 'case' for thinking of commonplace urban issues, debates and policies as happening at night-time and in dialogue with what takes place 'after hours'? In our short primer-like book, we have sought to encourage deeper historical and political insights, an appreciation of varied agendas and geographical experiences, and a look at those who make the NTE, not just those who consume it. In the spirit of practical applicability, therefore, we turn here to provide a practical closing guideline (we hesitate to call it a 'chapter' at this stage), structured around eight key lessons that we learned as scholars and practitioners of the night-time. We offer these as recommendations for both policymakers and others involved in this emerging field to consider. This is structured explicitly as a propositional list, pointing at a set of key successes, shortcomings and continuing inequalities, as well as some of what we think are practical ways past the COVID-19 crisis into a more effective (and inclusive) management of the night-time in cities. Underpinning all of these is the first proposition calling for formal recognition in policy in cities around the world, as well as the underlining normative stance that we call on policymakers and scholars to 'take a night stance' against daytime biases in practice and research. In doing so, we aim to conclude our short book as an open-ended, and yet hopefully also easily applied, call for attention to what happens after hours, seeking to inspire not just further socially minded research, but also, if not principally, progressive policy action.

Taking a night stance

Night studies and night-time governance are perhaps still in their infancy, or maybe their early adult years after a couple of decades of theoretical and practical development. Yet, as the previous chapters have sought to illustrate through repeated references to a large, and likely widening, variety of international experiences, they represent a thriving space for urban governance to engage with. From this standpoint, a few key issues emerge for us as central to pushing this evolution further. We have promoted a view that values the role of what happens after dark in understanding the broader landscape of how cities evolve. Ours has been an effort in highlighting the importance of accounting for whose livelihoods are at stake when we speak of NTEs, activities and atmospheres. We also highlighted how different interpretations of how the governance of the urban night works are driven not only by the pressures of local NTEs, but also by long-standing urban developmental trajectories that the cities have embarked on. We have done so in an explicit comparative sense to warn policymakers to consider how these might differ to their own cities ahead of simply importing overseas models for NTE management and, more broadly, urban governance. Rather, we advise starting from a set of eight practitioner-oriented propositions.

Our goal in this final chapter of the book is not so much to boil down the complexity of the NTE into a set of PowerPoint slides and catchy slogans. Rather, we turn to an explicitly assertive position designed not just as an introductory primer to night-time governance as per the rest of our volume, but also as a statement that has an explicit normative position about the value, complexity and lingering challenges of the night-time and cities. Through these propositions, we offer a summary of the main lessons emerging through the previous chapters, as well as in our own engagement with research, consultancy, policymaking and community action on the night-time dimensions of cities. We do so here, therefore, through the medium of a set of eight propositions acting as a quick reference guide on some of the key points of departure that we encourage night-time managers and researchers to take on board when venturing into the after hours of cities around the planet.

These are, of course, not just the result of our own deliberations or, indeed, just a summation of the case studies, vignettes and empirics outlined in Chapters 3, 4 and 5 of this book. Once again, we encourage a more fine-grained engagement with night studies and thinking, outlined in the 'further reading' and introductory parts of this book as a thriving realm of interdisciplinary discussions we believe of critical use not just to the academy, but to practitioners too. Fundamentally, the proposition summarized here takes the stance that we have been repeating throughout the book: seeking to encourage practitioners and researchers to veer away from perhaps more simplistic readings of what might account for night-time governance and embrace nuance in the possibilities open to the urban governance of what goes on after dark in cities. In the previous chapters, we encouraged a move away from the idea that there is a model that can be easily transferred from place to place to tackle NTE problems and growth. As we have illustrated, the governance of the night in cities is much broader than a single model. Even the role of the much-chronicled 'night mayor' is, in reality, a variety of different permutations based on complex circumstances, personal histories and intertwined public and private interests. We have advocated throughout the book for the need to ground our reading of the urban night in more contextual and specific governance considerations that are not blind to the historical trajectories that specific places might be embedded in, as well as the often-competing community, private sector and governmental interests that exist in the ways nightlife functions in cities the world over.

Yet, we have done so while also very clearly encouraging an urban governance approach that builds on current advancements in urban studies for the need to, as Jennifer Robinson (2011a) puts it, understand 'cities in a world of cities' and thus take up context-sensitive, nuanced, evidence-based, cosmopolitan and socially responsible 'comparative gestures' between cities (also see Robinson 2011b). We have hopefully shown in our explicitly internationalist approach how this can be a valuable starting point for urban policymakers and city governments as they look at each other for inspiration on how to shape the management of their urban lives after dark. Even in a context of deep crisis and a sustained rethinking of how our cities work in the wake of a global disruption such as that of COVID-19, the night-time presents opportunities for policymakers, scholars and non-governmental actors to better think, or even rethink, questions of inclusive urban development. From this perspective, the following eight propositions are centred on an explicit set of suggestions not for the sake of easy copycat policy mobility, but rather to provoke scholars and local governments (and, indeed, community and private sector advocates) to take a clear stance on what the value and purpose of the night-time is in their cities.

Our propositions

1. The night-time needs *an explicit role in urban governance*

Over the past decade, many cities have set up explicit structures to manage their night-time, ranging from mayors to councils, committees and offices. Yet, the work is far from over or far from common practice in local government. These experiences stress the value, challenges and potential of 'after-hours' thinking in urban policy, but much more is needed around the world. Night-time governance needs to be explicitly institutionalized in the way we manage cities. It requires purpose-fit institutions embedded in the apparatus of urban policymaking in cities, whether at the metropolitan, local or other scales, or ad hoc organizations that can overcome urban political limits that, at present, prevent cities from taking strategic action towards better night-time management. It also needs local policymakers (but also ideally their state and national counterparts) to explicitly recognize the night-time in those key agendas setting the direction of urban governance in cities the world over.

2. Governing the night is **not a single responsibility**

The urban night is not a homogeneous or uniform field. It does not adhere to a 'sector' and it entails a vast variety of interests, agendas and experiences that might not even be easily reconcilable. Individuals perceive and experience the night differently, and interpretations vary across different groups, such as women and migrant workers. This calls for a broader approach to night-time planning and design that, rather than being a top-down process dictated by strict regulations and policies, encourages the participation of different social actors and economic sectors. Continuous stakeholder and community consultation is vital, as is the need to have solid feet 'on the ground' of the nightlife realities experienced by all of those that inhabit it. Those who hold governmental responsibilities (for example, at the municipal level) or economic power (for example, in the 'core' NTE sectors) need to appreciate this variety and value not just economic outputs and return, but also the production side of the night-time, often made up of night-shift workers whose voices lag in policymaking, as well as the livelihoods side, often to do with vulnerable groups occupying the urban night in different ways.

3. Night-time **priorities vary greatly** from city to city and within cities

The case studies and cities analysed in this book reveal that priorities for cities vary considerably, which requires individualized strategies rather than a one-size-fits-all approach to night-time planning. While most 'night mayors' and night-time advocacy organizations share responsibility as mediators between local governments, residents and the nightlife industry, their scope and influence vary significantly based on local regulations, systems of governance and available resources to exercise the role. A copy-and-paste policy mobility approach will simply not do the trick for most. Night-time governance in a city must learn valuable lessons from other national and international counterparts, and aspire to do so on the basis of tangible evidence as to 'what works', but, at the same time, needs a serious (and evidence-based) appreciation of its own night-time scene(s). Equally, what might appear ideal to some (policymakers or otherwise) in one place might be at odds with the night-time needs of others – often marginal and silenced. Inclusive approaches, conscious of intersectional inequalities, are critical to any truly transformative after hours agenda.

4. The NTE is *a foundational economy*

The NTE encompasses more activities than those accounted for in gross domestic product (GDP) figures and contributes to the social reproduction of our urban societies and economies. If we are to design safe and inclusive night-time cities, then it is important to recognize that broader structural injustices shape who can choose to work or not at night, and who has agency or not over their working conditions. Without low-paid and often precariously employed night-time workers, our cities would stop functioning. Inclusive and progressive urban night-time management should attend to their needs, promoting policies that support low-income workers, such as subsidized public transport fares or minimum wage campaigns. Including carers, cleaners, sex workers and logistics workers in urban night decision-making and planning is essential. This can be achieved through partnerships with non-for-profit organizations that support often silenced or overshadowed groups, such as sex workers, alongside trade unions and other relevant representative bodies.

5. Enjoying the city at night remains *a privilege*

Your gender, age, race, physical condition and income still greatly shape whether or not you: will be able to afford to go out at night; will be welcomed in nightclubs, music venues and restaurants; will feel comfortable walking down the street or taking public transport; and can afford and access safe and reliable transport when you need it. More inclusive night-time strategies should take account of these patterns of inequalities and address them through adequate public realm interventions, careful public transport planning and anti-discrimination policies. Supporting night-time spaces that have historically played an important role in emancipatory struggles and in community building (for example, black cultural venues, LGBTQI+ venues and so on) through adequate planning policies (for example, rent caps and business support) is also essential. Once again, bringing urban equality considerations into approaches to NTE is essential, but also need to keep pace with an appreciation for the privileged position that night-time consumers have, and that certain night-time spaces afford, over others often less popularly chronicled.

6. Night-time economies can **reproduce broader injustices**

This means that urban night managers need to ask uncomfortable questions about what kind of NTEs they would like to promote. Do we want to collectively promote NTEs that create more precarious and low-paid jobs to support unsustainable, consumerist lifestyles? Or, would we rather promote, shape and celebrate inclusive NTEs where the value of essential care work and cultural activities are recognized, and where workers are supported through fair wages and access to adequate night-time infrastructures? Asking those questions also demands reflecting upon the value of keeping certain activities in the dark. Experiments with shifting cleaning schedules to the late afternoon instead of night-time or early morning, for instance, for cleaning staff working in municipally owned buildings, could be a first step to recognizing that essential work should be valued, recognized and not hidden from view. Campaigns to bring cleaning and security staff in-house, instead of hiring them via outsourced private companies, also offers avenues to think through how public institutions and ethical companies can value all workers equally.

7. Night-time **evidence is essential** to governing the afterhours, which cannot rely simply on daytime data and logics

The case for better attention to the NTE has typically been made on tangible economic statements about the size and impact of this activity on cities. There is now emerging proof from both conversations in night studies and practice that an explicit focus on evidence-based policy is critical to managing life at night in cities. This means not simply assuming an equation between what happens in daytime and the shape of the night in cities. Rather, this entails continuing reflexivity about what we think we know about the urban night and how to better understand this context. It also requires us to do so from the variety of lived experiences and viewpoints not just of the consumers of the night-time, but also of those who are busy producing and sustaining this economy. The flourishing of predominantly economic assessments of the NTE needs to go hand in hand with a broadening beyond economics. Night-time governance needs to be built on better information about the legal, sociocultural and design evidence that can more accurately cast what happens in cities at night-time and how this can also be managed in a socially inclusive, not just economically viable, way. Information about sustainability remains relatively scant, as is the balance between Global North experiences, which are now well accounted for in decades of writing about the NTE, and the still-sparse debate about Southern experiences, often available in languages other than English.

8. Governing the night means **taking responsibility for its sustainability**

Matching night-time concerns with sustainability imperatives requires us to strive for a broader reading of what happens after dark. The city is not just the realm of the NTE and its component sectors, and not just the realm of the lives and livelihoods that underpin that economy, but also a space that is critical to how urbanized human activity might, or might not, be sustainable in the long run. This means appreciating the environmental underpinnings of the expansion of '24/7' cities, for instance, as regards impinging on the flora and fauna that underpin our urban environments and their capacity to thrive alongside thriving cities. This entails taking up much more explicit considerations as to the sustainable development scorecard of cities and NTEs, as well as disaggregating contexts that might be deemed sustainable in general but perform very poorly when darkness falls upon our built environment and artificial lights go on.

Further Reading

Introduction

In this brief addendum, we offer a short guide to more literature that those interested, or working, in the night-time might find useful. We do so to stress once again that the field of night studies is thriving and expanding well beyond disciplinary boundaries, based between academia *and practice*, as well as to stress that 'non-traditional outputs' (as academic parlance puts it) are as valuable here as many excellent scholarly treatises. Practically, we present here a short, annotated bibliography of some samples from this burgeoning variety of material. We start with general introductions to night studies, and then follow on with specific investigations of night-time politics and planning. That is coupled with a note on current and recent (as of early 2021) night-time policy and non-governmental initiatives, as well as another reminder of the centrality that work on night-time inequalities plays in this field of research and action. In short, there are many terrific night scholars, advocates and practitioners out there that we strongly encourage the reader to go and meet for more after-hours explorations in the exciting, and socially urgent, spaces that night-time governance opens. We also encourage coupling these additional written sources with a short introductory podcast series that we produced, titled 'Cities After Dark' – available open access from the University of Melbourne's *Connected Cities* podcast on all major podcasting apps – for a hopefully insightful, more atmosphere-setting and conversational introduction to night-time studies that features many of the authors illustrated in the following.

A thriving literature (not just scholarship)

Our main goal in this primer has been to offer an accessible and practitioner-friendly introductory guide to the governance of cities at night-time. As noted and widely referenced throughout this volume, there are several texts already published to which this book can be placed as a companion. Some of these present important, if not foundational, readings in the literature, scholarly and otherwise, when it comes to 'night studies'. Of course, several of these books, reports and articles take either a specifically disciplinary standpoint or a particular normative stance in the context of their own scholarly debates and specific sociocultural contexts. Yet, as a whole, they clearly testify to a growing mass of valuable insights on night-time issues in cities. We focus here on pointing towards those that, in our view, are most directly connected to issues of urban *governance* at night, being conscious that the list would otherwise become an unwieldy mix and more than we could do justice to in our relatively limited-length primer.

Of course, those wishing to engage more widely with the night in cities could do so by building on an increasingly fertile ground. Scientific research on the night-time is scattered across academia and certainly ripe for a more holistic and cross-cutting engagement. Some disciplines have long-standing traditions of investigating specific night-time issues, and this is not just the purview of the social sciences. This is evident in many science, technology, engineering, mathematics and medicine (STEMM) areas (for example, Lee, 2013; Finkel, 2018), from work on the shifting circadian rhythms that govern our 'body clocks', to the bioscientific study of night-time animals (Davies et al, 2013). Experimental, albeit perhaps for the most part dissociated, work is emerging in the social sciences and humanities too, and the dialogue between these considerations and those in STEM areas has encouraging antecedents even in more public science debates, for instance, as in the dedicated special issues of *National Geographic* and *New Scientist* in 2018 and 2013, respectively. Geographers have turned to theorizing the impact of varying degrees of darkness on society, as well as to analysing night-time leisure (Chatterton and Hollands, 2003; Edensor, 2015; Gandy, 2017). Anthropological studies of night-time events like festivals and markets (for example, Jordan et al, 2004; Tinat, 2005) have been studied as an approach to understanding social dynamics. There is a long tradition in cultural studies of 'night walking' (Beaumont, 2015) and 'place hacking' (Garrett, 2013), as well as literature on darkness and the night. In short, there are plenty of interesting pockets of night-related research across a vast variety of disciplinary approaches. Here, we tease out a short collection of those more directly relevant for the discussions of our volume.

We do not intend the following list to be a definitive reader of night-time studies, for, as we underscore later, there are emerging collections far better placed than our confined effort within this specific volume. At the same time, we also encourage readers to make a concerted and explicit effort to hear and engage with the voices of those whose night-time experiences have taken place in the likes of Latin America, Africa, Asia, the Middle East and so forth, which, at times, are lacking from the major reference points of the literature in night studies. Likewise, we underscore here the important lesson that much of the discussion on night-time governance also requires us to keep up with academically non-traditional outputs. There are a plethora of examples beyond the more standard scholarly canons of books and journal articles that now speak to how the night-time practice (and studies) conversation is evolving. Rather, we would stress the importance of keeping an eye on and a keen ear towards alternative forms of national and international discussion, debate and exchange, as highlighted later. This is perhaps the most common shape of the current urban night debate beyond specific disciplinary economic policy interventions, and where most of the international encounter about the night-time takes place. In that spirit, as we flag later, we have also added a companion podcast series to this book, which both expands and takes a deeper dive into many of the issues and places discussed in the book. We have made the series publicly available free of charge and encourage the reader to consider the series and this volume to go hand in hand in our effort towards an introduction to night-time governance in cities.

General introductions to night-time studies

- Crary, J. (2013) *24/7: Late Capitalism and the Ends of Sleep*. London: Verso Books.
- Shaw, R. (2018) *The Nocturnal City*. London: Routledge.
- Dunn, N. and Edensor, T. (eds) (2020) *Rethinking Darkness: Cultures, Histories, Practices*. London: Routledge.

Night-time research, as noted earlier, spans widely across the academy. Within the specific context of cities-focused ('urban studies') or cities-relevant approaches that have dealt with the issues we tackle in this book, there are a few useful texts – of very different styles – that we would point the reader to. Crary's (2013) book is centred on the neoliberal colonization of the night-time by an increasingly '24/7' society. Shaw's (2018) more recent book is an in-depth discussion, with a quite extensive theoretical backing, of the 'frontier' quality of the night-time and the benefits of a 'nightology' for urban studies, in dialogue with discussions of 'planetary urbanization' (Brenner, 2014). It is also the one of these three with some important engagement with non-Western contexts (for example, Taiwan). All three embody elements of progressive critique that we embedded in several of our chapters and eight concluding propositions. Shaw's volume also offers an accessible summary of the development of the NTE tradition and its mainly UK-based roots, subjecting it to some useful critique as to the language and limitations it carries. Lastly, Dunn and Edensor's (2020) recent collection takes both a broader disciplinary angle as to night-time challenges and a more specific approach focusing more directly on the social, cultural and political underpinnings of darkness. It is also worth considering that a debate on what 'night studies' might be (or 'nightology' as Shaw puts it) has also led to a few recent pieces, including our own, on this front, for example:

- Gwiazdzinski, L., Maggioli, M. and Straw, W. (2018) Geographies of the night. From geographical object to night studies. *Bollettino della Società Geografica Italiana serie*, 14: 9–22.
- Acuto, M. (2019) We need a science of the night. *Nature*, 576(7787): 339.
- Kyba, C., Pritchard, S.B., Ekirch, A.R., Eldridge, A., Jechow, A., Preiser, C., Kunz, D., Henckel, D., Hölker, F., Barentine, J. and Berge, J. (2020) Night matters. Why the interdisciplinary field of 'night studies' is needed. *Multidisciplinary Scientific Journal*, 3(1): 1–6.

Gwiazdzinski, Maggioli and Straw's (2018) article offers a more specific reflection on the emergence of 'night studies' and how the discussions on cultural, political and material (and more) geographies of the night have been coalescing into a common conversation. We have engaged in this conversation ourselves (Acuto 2019) by stressing the need for a similar level of dialogue and experimentation across the STEMM–humanities–social sciences divides, with an eye on practical applicability – a theme of multidisciplinarity also picked up by Kyba and colleagues (2020), arguing as to why 'night studies' is needed today.

Investigations of night-time politics and planning

- Roberts, M. and Eldridge, A. (2012) *Planning the Night Time City*. London: Routledge.
- Hadfield, P. (2014) The night time city. Four modes of exclusion. *Urban Studies*, 52(3): 606–16 – and more generally the whole 2015 special issue of *Urban Studies* 52(3), entitled 'Geographies of the urban night'.
- Van Liempt, I. (2015) Safe nightlife collaborations: multiple actors, conflicting interests and different power distributions. *Urban Studies*, 52(3): 486–500.
- Kelly, H. (2016) *24 Hour Cities: Real Investment Performance, Not Just Promises*. London and New York, NY: Routledge.
- Wolifson, P. and Drozdzewski, D. (2017) Co-opting the night: the entrepreneurial shift and economic imperative in NTE planning. *Urban Policy and Research*, 35(4): 486–504.
- Mateo, J.N. and Eldridge, A. (eds) (2018) *Exploring Nightlife: Space, Society and Governance*. London: Rowman and Littlefield.

- Straw, W. (2018) Afterword: night mayors, policy mobilities and the question of night's end. In Mateo, J.N. and Eldridge, A (eds) *Exploring Nightlife: Space, Society and Governance*. London: Rowman & Littlefield, pp 225–31.
- Seijas, A. and Gelders, M.M. (2021) Governing the night time city: the rise of 'night mayors' as a new form of urban governance after dark. *Urban Studies*, 58(2), 316–334.

As noted in the first few chapters of this book, there is a solid track record of research and writing that tackles more specifically questions of the urban governance and planning of the NTE, or the night-time more generally. We suggest a few of these. Mateo and Eldridge's (2018) volume is perhaps the most recent counterpart to our effort and an important demonstration of the collegiality of the current night studies discussion. It is an edited collection centred on offering a variety of different disciplinary perspectives, mainly across the social sciences, as to 'nightlife'. Straw's afterword in this volume is particularly poignant for our book and conversation. Here, it stresses the global emergence of NTE governance, its underlying policy mobilities and agendas, and the need for greater attention on this front. Kelly's (2016) book is an example of a more practitioner-oriented volume, focused on US cities, thinking through what made for a 'recipe for success' in the post-nine-to-five economy of the last half-century. Roberts and Eldridge's (2012) volume, in turn, takes a more specific regulatory and planning focus, discussing issues like licensing at quite some depth (predominantly focused on the UK and other Western examples), presenting a now much-cited companion to the planning challenges of the NTE. Hadfield's (2014) commentary on a related *Urban Studies* special issue on 'Geographies of the urban night', guest edited by Ilse van Liempt, Irina van Aalst and Tim Schwanen, is a handy counterpart to this discussion, but we strongly encourage consulting the whole issue, rich in many of the key authors that we have cited and engaged with in this book. In particular, Van Liempt's (2015) article adds on to this a useful and more specific focus on the management style of NTE governance – a theme also tackled in Wolifson and Drozdzewski's (2017) more recent piece. We (Seijas and Gelders, 2021) have tackled this reality more explicitly in relation to the emergence of the 'night mayor' phenomenon and offered an initial comparative international assessment that partly inspired (and is reflected in) this volume.

Night-time policy and non-governmental initiatives

- Lam, F., Schwendinger, L., Luebkeman, C. and Hargrave, J. (2015) Rethinking the Shades of Night. Cities Alive Series Report. London: Arup.

Available at: www.arup.com/perspectives/publications/research/section/cities-alive-rethinking-the-shades-of-night
- Sound Diplomacy and Seijas, A. (2018) A guide to managing your night-time economy. July. Available at: www.sounddiplomacy.com/night-time-economy-guide
- Leichsenring, L., Milan, M. et al (2021) The Global Nighttime Recovery Plan. Available at: www.nighttime.org/recoveryplan/

Night-time advocacy has been thriving outside academia in the last decade. This is an important factor not to be understated when it comes to useful sources of updated information for scholars and practitioners alike, without, of course, diminishing the value of academia. From this point of view, a few resources stand out. UK-based consultancy Sound Diplomacy, with help from one of us, developed a 'guide' to managing the NTE in 2018 that is somewhat of a precursor to the approach we have taken here, reflecting a variety of snapshot case studies, in the Global South too. A few years earlier, international consultancy Arup put out a useful knowledge-based report as part of its Cities Alive series, aimed at grasping with more nuance the 'shades' of the night-time and the implications of not seeing the night as a simply monolithic entity. In our view, of course, this is imperative not only for urban design and lighting purposes, as that report was aimed at, but also for the broader sociocultural appreciation of the governance of the night-time as meaning many different things to many different stakeholders. More recently, and again with a few of us involved, a collective convened by Amsterdam/Berlin-based Vibe Lab developed a Global Nighttime Recovery Plan that exemplifies the collaborative and highly international nature of night-time practice and studies at present. The plan addresses various themes impacting night-time industries, not least with a dedicated chapter on governance, and is again freely available online (as are the other reports too). These are, of course, but three examples of the variety of useful documentation to be found out there in the thriving world of night-time advocacy and night-time studies, which we encourage readers to dive into.

Night-time inequalities

- Chatterton, P. and Hollands, R. (2003) *Urban Nightscapes: Youth Cultures, Pleasure Spaces and Corporate Power*. Hove: Psychology Press.
- Hobbs, D., Hadfield, P., Lister, S. and Winlow, S. (2003) *Bouncers: Violence and Governance in the Night Time Economy*. Oxford: Oxford University Press.
- Talbot, D. (2007) *Regulating the Night: Race, Culture and Exclusion in the Making of the Night Time Economy*. Farnham: Ashgate Publishing.

- Dunn, N. (2016) *Dark Matters: A Manifesto for the Nocturnal City.* London: John Hunt Publishing.
- Campkin, B. and Marshall, L. (2018) London's nocturnal queer geographies. *Soundings: A Journal of Politics and Culture,* 70: 82–96.
- Nicholls, E. (2018) *Negotiating Femininities in the Neoliberal Night Time Economy: Too Much of a Girl?* New York: Springer.

Questions surrounding inequality, the 'right to the night' and the impact of the NTE (and its governance) on particular social contexts are, as we have noted, critical to transforming NTE management into more progressive urban night-time governance. There is no shortage of excellent work on this front. Chatterton and Hollands' (2003) excursus on youth cultures, Hobbs et al's (2003) review of the securitization of entertainment in the NTE and Talbot's (2007) discussion of race and culture regulation are all sound examples of this.

The same goes for writing like Nicholls' (2018) book that offer particular stances, as with feminism, on how the neoliberal underpinnings of the NTE have affected urban life. That is also the more general theme of Dunn's (2016) manifesto, which echoes many of the issues raised in the previous section by Shaw (2018). We would also encourage engaging with the prolific and progressive debates emerging from work like that of Campkin and Marshall (2018), noted in our London case study, as to the particular impact of NTE management on LGBTQI+ (or 'queer') dimensions of nightlife, not just as to their role in entertainment and culture, but also so as to appreciate the possibilities for inclusion that a night studies conversation can encourage.

References

24horas.cl (2017) Las cinco medidas que pretende implanter el delegado nocturno de Valparaiso. 18 June. Available (in Spanish) at: www.24horas.cl/nacional/las-cinco-medidas-que-pretende-implantar-el-delegado-nocturno-de-valparaiso--2419954

Abadsidis, S. (2019) NYC is expecting 6 million visitors for the 50th anniversary of the Stonewall uprisings. *Gaynrd*, 31 May. Available at: www.gaynrd.com/nyc-expecting/

Abenoza, R.F., Ceccato, V., Susilo, Y.O. and Cats, O. (2018) Individual, travel, and bus stop characteristics influencing travelers' safety perceptions. *Transportation Research Record*, 2672(8): 19–28.

Acuto, M. (2010) High-rise Dubai urban entrepreneurialism and the technology of symbolic power. *Cities*, 27(4): 272–84.

Acuto, M. (2013) *Global Cities, Governance and Diplomacy: The Urban Link.* London: Routledge.

Acuto, M. (2019) We need a science of the night. *Nature*, 576(7787): 339.

Acuto, M. and Leffel, B. (2020) Understanding the global ecosystem of city networks. *Urban Studies*, 58(9): 1758-1774 .

Amsterdam (2018) Nacthraad [Night Council]. Available (in Dutch) at: https://nachtburgemeester.amsterdam/Nachtraad

Bader, I. and Scharenberg, A. (2010) The sound of Berlin: subculture and the global music industry. *International Journal of Urban and Regional Research*, 34(1): 76–91.

Baer, D. (2016) Amsterdam's 'night mayor' is turning his city into a 24-hour adventure. February. Available at: www.businessinsider.com/mirik-milan-amsterdam-night-mayor-2016-2/?r=AU&IR=T

Barrie, I. (2015) Not going out: why millennials are no longer going to night clubs. Available at: www.independent.co.uk/arts-entertainment/music/features/not-going-out-why-millennials-are-no-longer-going-to-night-clubs-10449036.html

Beaumont, M. (2015) *Nightwalking.* London: Verso.

Beer, C. (2011) Centres that never sleep? Planning for the night time economy within the commercial centres of Australian cities. *Australian Planner*, 48(3): 141–7.

Bennett, T. (2020) The justification of a music city: handbooks, intermediaries and value disputes in a global policy assemblage. *City, Culture and Society*, 22: 100354.

Bianchini, F. (1995) Night cultures, night economies. *Planning Practice and Research*, 10(2): 121–6.

Blanco, I. (2013) Analysing urban governance networks: bringing regime theory back in. *Environment and Planning C: Government and Policy*, 31(2): 276–91.

Boscia, S. (2019) London Night Tube crime rates soar in 2018–19. *City A.M.*, 14 October. Available at: www.cityam.com/london-night-tube-crime-rates-soar-in-2018-19/

Brands, J., Schwanen, T. and Van Aalst, I. (2015) Fear of crime and affective ambiguities in the night time economy. *Urban Studies*, 52(3): 439–55.

Bray, J. and Bellamy, S. (2019) What's driving bus patronage change? Research report. Urban Transport Group. Available at: https://www.urbantransportgroup.org/resources/types/reports/whats-driving-bus-patronage-change-analysis-evidence-base

Brenner, N. (ed) (2014) *Implosions/Explosions. Towards a Study of Planetary Urbanization*. Berlin: Jovis.

Broadgate (2019) What to see at Pride London 2019. Available at: www.broadgate.co.uk/event/what-to-see-at-pride-london-2019

Browne, R. (2020a) Uber fights London ban in court for the second time. *CNBC News*, 14 September. Available at: www.cnbc.com/2020/09/14/uber-fights-london-ban-in-court-for-a-second-time.html

Browne, R. (2020b) Uber granted 19-month London license as judge overturns ban. *CBNC News*, 28 September. Available at: www.cnbc.com/2020/09/28/uber-granted-temporary-london-license.html

Bunnell, T. (2015) Antecedent cities and inter-referencing effects: learning from and extending beyond critiques of neoliberalisation. *Urban Studies*, 52(11): 1983–2000.

Campkin, B. and Marshall, L. (2017) *LGBTQ+ Cultural Infrastructure in London: Night Venues, 2006–Present*. London: UCL Urban Laboratory.

Campkin, B. and Marshall, L. (2018) London's nocturnal queer geographies. *Soundings: A Journal of Politics and Culture*, 70: 82–96.

Chatterton, P. and Hollands, R. (2002) Theorising urban playscapes: producing, regulating and consuming youthful nightlife city spaces. *Urban Studies*, 39(1): 95–116.

Chatterton, P. and Hollands, R. (2003) *Urban Nightscapes: Youth Cultures, Pleasure Spaces and Corporate Power*. London: Psychology Press.

City and County of San Francisco (2020) Residential development compatibility. Entertainment Commission. Available at: https://sfgov.org/entertainment/residential-development-compatibility

Coldwell, W. (2016) Fabric to close this weekend after drug-related deaths. *The Guardian*, 11 August. Available at: www.theguardian.com/uk-news/2016/aug/11/fabric-london-nightclub-close-weekend-deaths-teenagers

Colomb, C. (2013) *Staging the New Berlin: Place Marketing and the Politics of Urban Reinvention Post-1989.* Abingdon: Routledge.

Committee for Sydney (2018) *Sydney as a 24-hour City.* Available at: https://www.sydney.org.au/wp-content/uploads/2018/12/CFS_Sydney-24hr-City_SINGLES_WEB_V11.pdf.

Crary, J. (2013) *24/7: Late Capitalism and the Ends of Sleep.* London: Verso Books.

Crawford, A. and Flint, J. (2009) Urban safety, anti-social behaviour and the night time economy. *Criminology & Criminal Justice*, 9(4): 403–13.

Da Cruz, N., Rode, P. and McQuarrie, M. (2019) New urban governance: a review of current themes and future priorities. *Journal of Urban Affairs*, 41(1): 1–19.

Dammert Guardia, M. (2007) La hora zanahoria (Internacional). *Ciudad segura. Programa de Estudios de la Ciudad. Cronología de la violencia* [Safe city. Research Program on the City. Chronology of the violence], 14(February): 3.

Davidson, K., Coenen, L., Acuto, M. and Gleeson, B. (2020) Reconfiguring urban governance in an age of rising city networks: A research agenda. *Urban studies*, 56(16): 3540–55.

Davies, T.W., Bennie, J., Inger, R. and Gaston, K.J. (2013) Artificial light alters natural regimes of night time sky brightness. *Scientific Reports*, 3: 1722.

Dunn, N. and Edensor, T. (eds) (2020) *Rethinking Darkness: Cultures, Histories, Practices.* London: Routledge.

Edensor, T. (2015) The gloomy city: rethinking the relationship between light and dark. *Urban Studies*, 52(3): 422–38.

Ernst & Young and London First (2016) London's 24-hour economy: the economic value of London's 24 hour economy. Available at: https://www.londonfirst.co.uk/sites/default/files/documents/2018-05/Londons-24-hour-economy.pdf

Fainstein, S., Gordon, I. and Harloe, M. (2011) Ups and downs in the global city: London and New York in the twenty-first century. In Bridge, G. and Watson, S. (eds) *The New Blackwell Companion to the City.* Oxford: Blackwell Publishing.

Finkel, M. (2018) While we sleep, our mind goes on an amazing journey. *National Geographic*, August.

Fort Lauderdale (2018) City of Fort Lauderdale FY preliminary budget. City Manager's Office, Fort Lauderdale. Available at: www.fortlauderdale.gov/Home/ShowDocument?id=22575

Füller, H., Helbrecht, I., Schlüter, S., Mackrodt, U., van Gielle Ruppe, P., Genz, C., and Dirksmeier, P. (2018) Manufacturing marginality.(Un-) governing the night in Berlin. *Geoforum*, 94, 24–32.

Futamura, T. and Sugiyama, K. (2018) The dark side of the nightscape: the growth of izakaya chains and the changing landscapes of evening eateries in Japanese cities. *Food, Culture & Society*, 21(1): 101–17.

Gandy, M. (2017) Negative luminescence. *Annals of the American Association of Geographers*, 107(5): 1090–107.

Garcia, L.-M. (2018) Agonistic festivities: urban nightlife scenes and the sociability of 'anti-social' fun. *Annals of Leisure Research*, 21(4): 462–79.

Garrett, B. (2013) *Explore Everything*. London: Verso.

Gelder, S. (2019) Hackney Council licensing policy row: campaigners granted judicial review of unpopular decision. *Hackney Gazette*, 26 March. Available at: www.hackneygazette.co.uk/news/hackney-council-licensing-policy-row-campaigners-granted-judicial-review-of-3622092

Geneva (2018) Grand Conseil de la Nuit [Great Council of the Night]. Available at: http://grandconseildelanuit.ch/

GLA (2015) *London's Grassroots Music Venues Rescue Plan*. London: Greater London Authority.

GLA (2017a) *From Good Night to Great Night. A Vision for London as a 24-Hour City*. London: Greater London Authority. Available at: www.london.gov.uk/sites/default/files/24_hour_london_vision.pdf

GLA (2017b) Culture and the night time economy: supplementary planning guidance. April. Available at: www.london.gov.uk/sites/default/files/ntc_spg_2017_a4_public_consultation_report_fa_0.pdf

GLA (2018a) London from 6pm to 6am. March. Available at: www.london.gov.uk/city-hall-blog/london-6pm-6am

GLA (2018b) The Night Tube. Available at: www.london.gov.uk/transport/rail-and-underground/night-tube

GLA (2018c) Night Tube is even bigger success than predicted, new figures show. Press release, August. Available at: www.london.gov.uk/press-releases/mayoral/night-tube-is-even-bigger-success-than-predicted

Gleeson, B. (2014). *The Urban Condition*. London: Routledge.

Gornostaeva, G. and Campbell, N. (2012) The creative underclass in the production of place: example of Camden Town in London. *Journal of Urban Affairs*, 34(2): 169–88.

Greco, D. (2019) Keeping Orlando moving through the night. *Cities at Night*, 30 August, New Cities. Available at: https://newcities.org/the-big-picture-keeping-orlando-moving-through-the-night/

Gwiazdzinski, L., Maggioli, M. and Straw, W. (2018) Geographies of the night. From geographical object to night studies. *Bollettino della Società Geografica Italiana*, 14: 9–22.

Hackney Council (2018) Licensing consultation report. 31 January. Available at: https://consultation.hackney.gov.uk/licensing/licensing-policy-consultation/results/licensingconsultationreport.pdf

Hadfield, P. (2014) The night time city. Four modes of exclusion. *Urban Studies*, 52(3): 606–16.

Hadfield, P., Lister, S. and Traynor, P. (2009) 'This town's a different town today': Policing and regulating the night time economy. *Criminology & Criminal Justice*, 9(4): 465–85.

Hae, L. (2011). Dilemmas of the nightlife fix: Post-industrialisation and the gentrification of nightlife in New York City. *Urban Studies*, 48(16): 3449-3465.

Hae, L. (2012). *The gentrification of nightlife and the right to the city: Regulating spaces of social dancing in New York*. New York: Routledge.

Harnden, A. (2017) Night time economy 2017 goals. Available at: https://heinz.campusgroups.com/icmasc/get_file?eid=8c8608f476bb0adbca1aac319af38817

Harris, J. (2015) End of the party: how police and councils are calling time on Britain's nightlife. *The Guardian*, 26 June. Available at: https://www.theguardian.com/music/2015/jun/26/fight-for-britains-nightlife-police-council-strangling-night-time-economy

Hawthorn, C. (2020) Amsterdam 'night mayor' Shamiro van der Geld replaced after leaving post in June 2019. *Resident Advisor*, 12 February. Available at: www.residentadvisor.net/news/71934

Hobbs, D., Hadfield, P., Lister, S. and Winlow, S. (2003) *Bouncers: Violence and Governance in the Night Time Economy*. Oxford: Oxford University Press.

Hobbs, R.F., Winlow, S., Hadfield, P. and Lister, S. (2005) Violent hypocrisy: governance and the night time economy. *European Journal of Criminology*, 2(2): 161–83.

Homan, S. (2019) Lockout laws or 'rock out' laws? Governing Sydney's night time economy and implications for the music city. *International Journal of Cultural Policy*, 25(4): 500–14.

Hopkins, G.R., Gaston, K.J., Visser, M.E., Elgar, M.A. and Jones, T.M. (2018) Artificial light at night as a driver of evolution across urban–rural landscapes. *Frontiers in Ecology and the Environment*, 16(8): 472–9.

Hoscik, M. (2018) TfL confirms plans to axe or shorten dozens of London bus routes. *MayorWatch*, 28 September. Available at: www.mayorwatch.co.uk/tfl-confirms-plans-to-axe-of-shorten-dozens-of-london-bus-routes/

Ingenium Research (2018) Measuring the Australian night time economy 2016–2017. Report for the Council of Capital Cities Lord Mayors (CCCLM), 14 September. Available at: www.lordmayors.org/wp-content/uploads/2018/09/Measuring-the-Australian-NTE_2016-17_FINAL_2018-09-14-1.pdf

Islington Council (2016) Joint statement by the London Borough of Islington and Fabric Life Limited. Press release. London Borough of Islington, UK.

Jones, D. (2018) 'This is not a curfew' – Hackney Mayor responds to restrictive new licensing laws. *NME*, 27 July. Available at: www.nme.com/news/this-is-not-a-curfew-hackney-mayor-responds-to-restrictive-new-legislation-2360253

Jordan, D.K., Morris, A.D. and Moskowitz, M.L. (eds) (2004) *The Minor Arts of Daily Life: Popular Culture in Taiwan*. Honolulu: University of Hawaii Press.

Kabala, J. and Robin, E. (2020) *Night Shifts*. Documentary film available upon demand.

Kadokura, T. (2007) Japan's underground economy. *The Japanese Economy*, 34(2): 20–49.

Katz, C. (2001) Vagabond capitalism and the necessity of social reproduction. *Antipode*, 33(4): 709–28.

Khan, S. (2016) Mayor of London's response to decision to revoke Fabric's licence. Press release, Mayor of London. Available at: https://www.london.gov.uk/press-releases/mayoral/fabrics-licence-revoked

Kolioulis, A. (2018) More day in the night? The gentrification of London's night time through clubbing. *Bollettino della Società Geografica Italiana*, 14(1–2): 207–18.

Kolioulis, A. (2020) The impact of COVID-19 on night-time economies, arts and culture. Blog, UCL Bartlett 'Post COVID-19 Urban Futures' series, 30 June. Available at: https://blogs.ucl.ac.uk/dpublog/2020/06/30/the-impact-of-covid-19-on-night-time-economies-arts-and-culture/

Koren, T. (2018) 24-hour clubs can totally transform a city, both for better and for worse. February. Available at: https://noisey.vice.com/en_uk/article/a3ndkp/24-hour-clubs-amsterdam-nightlife-2018

Koslofsky, C. (2011) *Evening's Empire: A History of the Night in Early Modern Europe (New Studies in European History)*. Cambridge and New York, NY: Cambridge University Press.

Kyba, C., Pritchard, S.B., Ekirch, A.R., Eldridge, A., Jechow, A., Preiser, C., Kunz, D., Henckel, D., Hölker, F., Barentine, J. and Berge, J. (2020) Night matters. Why the interdisciplinary field of 'night studies' is needed. *Multidisciplinary Scientific Journal*, 3(1): 1–6.

Lagadic, M. (2019) Along the London Overground: transport improvements, gentrification, and symbolic ownership along London's trendiest line. *City & Community*, 18(3): 1003–27.

Lam, F., Schwendinger, L., Luebkeman, C. and Hargrave, J. (2015) *Rethinking the Shades of Night. Cities Alive Series Report*. London: Arup. Available at: www.arup.com/perspectives/publications/research/section/cities-alive-rethinking-the-shades-of-night

Landry, C. (2000) *The Creative City: A Toolkit for Urban Innovators*. London: Earthscan.

Lauermann, J. (2018) Municipal statecraft: revisiting the geographies of the entrepreneurial city. *Progress in Human Geography*, 42(2): 205–24.

Lee, J.J. (2013) Marine animals keep time with multiple clocks. *National Geographic*, September.

Lee, M., Tomsen, S. and Wadds, P. (2020) Locking-out uncertainty: conflict and risk in Sydney's night time economy. In Pratt, J. and Anderson, J. (eds) *Criminal Justice, Risk and the Revolt against Uncertainty*. London: Springer Nature, pp 191–215.

London Night Time Commission (2018) *Think Night: London's Neighbourhoods from 6pm to 6am*. London: Mayor's Office.

Lovatt, A. and O'Connor, J. (1995) Cities and the night time economy. *Planning Practice & Research*, 10(2): 127–34.

MacQuarie, J.C. (2017a) Invisible denizens: migrant night shift workers' fragile possibilities for solidarity in the post-circadian capitalist era. Working Paper Series 2017/4, Centre for Policy Studies, Central European University. Available at: https://cps.ceu.edu/publications/working-paper/invisible-denizens-migrant-night-shift-workers-fragile-possibilities

MacQuarie, J. C. (2017b). *Invisible Migrants*. Doctoral dissertation, Central European University.

Mateo, J.N. and Eldridge, A. (eds) (2018) *Exploring Nightlife: Space, Society and Governance*. London: Rowman & Littlefield.

McArthur, J. (2019) The production and politics of urban knowledge: contesting transport in Auckland, New Zealand. *Urban Policy and Research*, 37(1): 45–61.

McArthur, J., Robin, E. and Smeds, E. (2019) Socio-spatial and temporal dimensions of transport equity for London's night time economy. *Transportation Research Part A: Policy and Practice*, 121: 433–43.

McCann, E. and Ward, K. (2014) Exploring urban policy mobilities: the case of business improvement districts. *Sociologica*, 8(1): 1-10.

McGranahan, G., & Satterthwaite, D. (2014). *Urbanisation Concepts and Trends*. London: International Institute for Environment and Development.

Melbourne, City of (2014) Beyond safe city strategy. City of Melbourne. Available at: www.melbourne.vic.gov.au/SiteCollectionDocuments/beyond-safe-city-strategy-2014.pdf

Melbourne, City of (2020) Night-time Economy Advisory Committee. City of Melbourne. Available at: https://www.melbourne.vic.gov.au/about-council/committees-meetings/Pages/night-time-economy-advisory-committee.aspx

Merkel, J. (2012) Creative governance in Berlin. In Anheier, H. K., and Isar, Y. R. (eds) *Cultures and Globalization: Cities, Cultural Policy and Governance.* London: Sage, pp 160–166.

Nantes (2016) Vivre Nantes la nuit. [Living at night]. December. Available at: www.johannarolland.fr/2016/12/16/vivre-nantes-la-nuit/

Neate, R. (2014) Berlin's "poor but sexy" appeal turning city into European Silicon Valley. *The Guardian*, 4 January, available at: *https://www.theguardian. com/business/2014/jan/03/berlin-poor-sexy-silicon-valley-microsoft-google*

New South Wales Government (2020) *Greater Sydney 24-hour Economy Strategy.* Available at: https://www.investment.nsw.gov.au/greater-sydneys-24-hour-economy/

New York City Government (2019) *NYC's Nightlife Economy.* Available at: https://www1.nyc.gov/site/mome/nightlife/economic-impact-study.page

New York State Liquor Authority (2020) Guidance on restrictions for licensees and to-go and delivery sales in response to COVID-19 outbreak. Available at: https://sla.ny.gov/Restrictions-in-Response-to-COVID-19

Nicholls, E. (2018) *Negotiating Femininities in the Neoliberal Night Time Economy: Too Much of a Girl?* New York: Springer.

Nicholson, R. (2016) Drugs, developers and diplomacy: London night tsar Amy Lamé on the challenges of the job. *The Guardian*, 10 December.

Norris, C., McCahill, M. and Wood, D. (2004) The growth of CCTV: a global perspective on the international diffusion of video surveillance in publicly accessible space. *Surveillance & Society*, 2: 110–35.

O'Mahony, D. and Orrell, H. (2017) Ban on Uber will cost us 10% of our trade, say bars and restaurants. *The Evening Standard*, 25 September.

Oviedo Hernandez, D. and Titheridge, H. (2016) Mobilities of the periphery: informality, access and social exclusion in the urban fringe in Colombia. *Journal of Transport Geography*, 55: 152–64.

Paris (2018) Manifeste Parisien sur la vie nocturne [Parisian Manifesto on Night Life]. Available (in French) at: www.paris.fr/municipalite/action-municipale/manifeste-parisien-sur-la-vie-nocturne-4569

Parnell, S. (2016) Defining a global urban development agenda. *World Development*, 78: 529–540.

Parnell, S. and Robinson, J. (2017) The global urban: difference and complexity in urban studies and the science of cities. In Hall, S. and Burdett, R. (eds). London *The Sage Handbook of the 21st Century City*, Sage, pp 13–31.

Peck, J. (2011) Geographies of policy: from transfer-diffusion to mobility-mutation. *Progress in Human Geography*, 35(6): 773–97.

Pereira, R., Schwanen, T. and Banister, D. (2017) Distributive justice and equity in transportation. *Transport Reviews*, 37(2): 170–91.

Phelps, N.A. and Miao, J.T. (2020) Varieties of urban entrepreneurialism. *Dialogues in Human Geography*, 10(3): 304–21.

Pieroni, R. (2015) The institutionalization of the night: a geography of Geneva's night policies. *Articulo – Journal of Urban Research*, 11, available at: https://journals.openedition.org/articulo/3147

Pierre, J. (2011) *The Politics of Urban Governance*. Basingstoke: Palgrave Macmillan.

Plyushteva, A. (2019). Commuting and the urban night: Nocturnal mobilities in tourism and hospitality work. *Journal of Policy Research in Tourism, Leisure and Events*, 11(3): 407–421.

Rennes (2016) Charte de la vie nocturne: Passons la nuit ensemble. [Night Life Charter] City of Rennes, February.

RHI (Responsible Hospitality Institute) (2018) Home page. Available at: www.rhiweb.org/

Rapoport, E., Acuto, M. Grcheva, L. (2019) *Leading cities: a global review of city leadership*. London: University College London Press.

Roberts, M. (2006) From 'creative city' to 'no-go areas' – the expansion of the night time economy in British town and city centres. *Cities*, 23(5): 331–8.

Roberts, M. (2009) Planning, urban design and the night time city: still at the margins? *Criminology and Criminal Justice*, 9(4): 487–506.

Roberts, M. (2018) 'Agent of Change' protects music venues from noise complaints, but won't stop them from closing. January. Available at: https://theconversation.com/agent-of-change-protects-music-venues-from-noise-complaints-but-wont-stop-them-from-closing-90556

Roberts, M. and Eldridge, A. (2008) Town planning and the night-time city: still at the margins. Presentation at the ESRC Seminar Series, 'Anti-Social Behaviour, Urban Spaces and the Night Time Economy', University of Leeds, April. Available at: https://essl.leeds.ac.uk/law-research-expertise/events/event/760/esrc-seminar-series-anti-social-behaviour-urban-spaces-and-the-night-time-economy

Roberts, M. and Eldridge, A. (2012) *Planning the Night Time City*. London: Routledge.

Robin, E. (2018) Performing real estate value(s): real estate developers, systems of expertise and the production of space. *Geoforum*. Available at https://doi.org/10.1016/j.geoforum.2018.05.006

Robin, E. and Acuto, M. (2018) Global urban policy and the geopolitics of urban data. *Political Geography*, 66: 76–87.

Robin, E. and Charpentier, L. (2019) A night in the life of London's night time workers. London: University College London. Available at: https://docs.wixstatic.com/ugd/69d120_36532c3dc52a4c04886b5c7ee872606a.pdf

Robin, E., Smeds, E. and McArthur, J. (2017) Nurses, drivers and delivery people: meet the real stars of the night time economy. *The Conversation*, 17 October. Available at: https://theconversation.com/nurses-drivers-and-delivery-people-meet-the-real-stars-of-the-night-time-economy-85340

Robinson, J. (2011a) Cities in a world of cities: the comparative gesture. *International Journal of Urban and Regional Research*, 35(1): 1–23.

Robinson, J. (2011b). Comparisons: colonial or cosmopolitan?. *Singapore Journal of Tropical Geography*, 32(2): 125-140.

Rowe, D. and Lynch, R. (2012) Work and play in the city: some reflections on the night time leisure economy of Sydney. *Annals of Leisure Research*, 15(2): 132–47.

Schwanen, T., Van Aalst, I., Brands, J., and Timan, T. (2012) Rhythms of the night: spatiotemporal inequalities in the nighttime economy. *Environment and Planning A*, 44(9), 2064–2085.

Seijas, A. (2019) *A Manifesto for Nocturnal Cities in Latin America*. London: Sound Diplomacy. Available at: https://www.academia.edu/40007092/Latin_American_Nocturnal_Cities_Manifesto

Seijas, A. (2020a) Nocturnal heritage: awakening the Historic Quarter of Valparaiso. *Latin America Policy Journal*, 9(Spring): 71–9.

Seijas, A. (2020b) Governing the urban night: understanding the shifting dynamics of night time governance in three global cities. Doctoral dissertation, Harvard Graduate School of Design, ProQuest Dissertations Publishing, Publication No. 28154794.

Seijas, A. and Gelders, M. (2021) Governing the night time city: the rise of 'night mayors' as a new form of urban governance after dark. *Urban Studies*, 58(2): 316–334.

Shaw, R. (2010) Neoliberal subjectivities and the development of the night time economy in British cities. *Geography Compass*, 4(7): 893–903.

Shaw, R. (2014) Beyond night time economy: affective atmospheres of the urban night. *Geoforum*, 51: 87–95.

Shaw, R. (2015) Night as fragmenting frontier: understanding the night that remains in an era of 24/7. *Geography Compass*, 9(12): 637–47.

Shaw, R. (2018) *The Nocturnal City*. London: Routledge.

Sheller, M. (2018) *Mobility Justice: The Politics of Movement in an Age of Extremes*. London and New York, NY: Verso.

Sheridan, D. (2007) The space of subculture in the city: getting specific about Berlin's indeterminate territories. *Journal of Architecture*, 1(1): 97–119.

Sheridan, E. (2019) Judicial review of Hackney's controversial licensing policy 'struck out'. *Hackney Citizen*, 5 June. Available at: www.hackneycitizen.co.uk/2019/06/05/judicial-review-hackneys-controversial-licensing-policy-struck-out/

Sisson, P. (2016) How night mayors are proving the economic and cultural value of robust nightlife. *Curbed.com*, 6 September, Available at: https://www.curbed.com/2016/9/6/12814920/club-nightlife-dance-music-night-mayor-club-commission

Sisson, A. and Maginn, P. (2018) 'Sanitised' nightlife precincts become places where some are not welcome, *The Conversation*, 10 May. Available at: https://theconversation.com/sanitised-nightlife-precincts-become-places-where-some-are-not-welcome-95870

Smeds, E., Robin, E. and McArthur, J. (2020) Night time mobilities and (in)justice in London: constructing mobile subjects and the politics of difference in policy-making. *Journal of Transport Geography*, 82: 102569.

Sound Diplomacy and Seijas, A. (2018) A guide to managing your night time economy. July. Available at: www.sounddiplomacy.com/night-time-economy-guide/

Stichting Nachtburgemeester Amsterdam (2018) About the 'night mayor' of Amsterdam. Available at: https://nachtburgemeester.amsterdam/English

Stichting Nachtburgemeester Amsterdam (2020) Dit zijn d zes nieuwe 24-uurslocaties [These are the six new 24-hour locations]. 10 June. Available (in Dutch) at: https://nachtburgemeester.amsterdam/Dit-zijn-de-zes-nieuwe-24-uurslocaties

Straw, W. (2018) Afterword: night mayors, policy mobilities and the question of night's end. In Mateo, J.N. and Eldridge, A. (eds) *Exploring Nightlife: Space, Society and Governance*. London: Rowman & Littlefield, pp 225–31.

Sullivan, C. and Pickard, J. (2015) TfL faces £700m a year cut in state subsidy by turn of the decade. *Financial Times*, 12 November.

Sydney, City of (2007) *Late Night Trading Premises Development Control Plan*. Available at: https://www.cityofsydney.nsw.gov.au/development-control-plans/late-night-trading-premises-dcp-2007

Sydney, City of (2011) Open directions: final report. City of Sydney, October. Available at: www.cityofsydney.nsw.gov.au/__data/assets/pdf_file/0018/131715/OpenDirectionsReportFinal.pdf

Sydney, City of (2020) Nightlife and Creative Sector Advisory Panel. Available at: https://www.cityofsydney.nsw.gov.au/advisory-panels/nightlife-creative-sector-advisory-panel

Talbot, D. (2004) Regulation and racial differentiation in the construction of night time economies: a London case study. *Urban Studies*, 41(4): 887–901.

Talbot, D. (2006) The Licensing Act 2003 and the problematization of the night time economy: planning, licensing and subcultural closure in the UK. *International Journal of Urban and Regional Research*, 30(1): 159–71.

Talbot, D. (2007) *Regulating the Night: Race, Culture and Exclusion in the Making of the Night Time Economy*. Farnham: Ashgate Publishing

Talbot, D. and Böse, M. (2007) Racism, criminalization and the development of night time economies: two case studies in London and Manchester. *Ethnic and Racial Studies*, 30(1): 95–118.

Tinat, K. (2005) The Spanish fiesta: the theatricality of a night club in Madrid. *Paideuma*, 51: 235–45.

Toronto (2018) Night time economy – stakeholder consultation results and next steps. Toronto City, March. Available at: www.toronto.ca/legdocs/mmis/2018/ed/bgrd/backgroundfile-113762.pdf

Van Liempt, I. (2015) Safe nightlife collaborations: multiple actors, conflicting interests and different power distributions. *Urban Studies*, 52(3): 486–500.

Vergès, F. (2019) Capitalocene, waste, race, and gender. *e-flux*. Available at: www.e-flux.com/journal/100/269165/capitalocene-waste-race-and-gender/

Wadds, P. (2020) *Policing Nightlife*. London: Routledge.

Walker, A. (2018) London bus cuts to hit working-class hardest, says watchdog. *The Guardian*, 18 August. Available at: www.theguardian.com/uk-news/2018/aug/18/london-bus-cuts-to-hit-working-class-hardest-says-watchdog

Welsh, B.C. and Farrington, D.P. (2003) The effects of closed-circuit television on crime. *The ANNALS of the American Academy of Political and Social Science*, 587(1): 110–35.

Williams, R. (2008) Night spaces: darkness, deterritorialization, and social control. *Space and Culture*, 11: 514–32.

Willoughby, I. (2019) Prague 'night mayor' Jan Štern: tourists often don't realize 'party zones' are residential areas. *Radio Prague International*, 19 August. Available at: www.radio.cz/en/section/one-on-one/prague-night-mayor-jan-stern-tourists-often-dont-realise-party-zones-are-residential-areas

WLH (We Love Hackney) (2018) The campaign to keep Hackney happening. Available at: https://www.lovehackney.uk

Wolifson, P. (2018) 'Civilising' by gentrifying: the contradictions of neoliberal planning for nightlife in Sydney, Australia. In Mateo, J.N. and Eldridge, A. (eds) *Exploring Nightlife: Space, Society and Governance*. Lanham: Rowman & Littlefield, pp 35–52.

Wolifson, P. and Drozdzewski, D. (2017) Co-opting the night: the entrepreneurial shift and economic imperative in NTE planning. *Urban Policy and Research*, 35(4): 486–504.

Yavuz, N. and Welch, E.W. (2010) Addressing fear of crime in public space: gender differences in reaction to safety measures in train transit. *Urban Studies*, 47(12): 2491–515.

Yeo, S.J. (2020) Right to the city (at night): Spectacle and surveillance in public space. In Mehta, V., and Palazzo, D. (eds.) *Companion to Public Space*. New York: Routledge, pp. 182–190.

Young, I.M. (2011 [1990]) *Justice and the Politics of Difference* (2011 edn). Princeton, NJ: Princeton University Press.

Index

Note: References to figures appear in *italic* type;
those in **bold** type refer to tables.

A

Aberdeen, UK 29, 36
accreditations 13
Acuto, M. 7, 18, 20, 95n1, 114
advocacy, night-time 84, 99, 107, 116
  global distribution of organizations 17, *19*
  role of night mayors 15–17
  timeline of organizations *16*
agendas, night-time 74–84
  focusing on NTE 39–40, 77–9
  to night-time strategies 83–4
  noise, safety and crime 79–80
  transport and logistics 81–2
  workers 82–3
'agent of change' principle 58–9, 80
alcohol
  regulation *see* licensing policies
  -related crime and violence, limiting 55,
    71–2, 102
Amsterdam, Netherlands 32
  24-hour licence initiative 78, 102
  night council 32
  night mayor 3, 14–15, 32, 78
  Night Watch Conglomerate 14, 15, 32
  'square hosts' 13–14, 15, 79
Andrés Carne de Res 72
Arup 5, 115, 116
Asobares 72
Asociación de Locatarios Nocturnos
    de Valparaíso ('Nightlife Business
    Association of Valparaiso'
    [ALNOVAL]) 71
Asunción, Paraguay 32–3, 72, 80
Australia
  Ballarat 59
  Yarra 53, 58, 59
  see also Melbourne, Australia;
    Sydney, Australia

B

Berlin, Germany 33, 62, 67–9

Club Commission 3, 6, 14, 15, 33, 68, 69
best-practices 13, 51, 52, 77, 79
black cultural venues 44, 89, 108
boards, advisory 26, 27, 36, 50–1, 52
Bogota, Colombia 62–3, 71–3, 80
  'Carrot Law' (*Ley Zanahoria*) 71–2
  'Nocturnal Cities' conference 73
  project to revitalize *Zona Rosa* 73
  Responsible Partying' (*Farra en la Buena*) 73
  Safe Seal (*Sello Seguro*) 72–3
Böse, M. 89

C

C40 Cities 57
'Cabaret Law' 51, 52
Cali, Colombia 29, 72
Campkin, B. 44, 89, 117
Canada
  Montreal 33–4
  Toronto 98
capacity-building role of night mayors 17
Capp, S. 60
'Carrot Law' (*Ley Zanahoria*) 71–2
CCTV 12
charters, nightlife 14
  London **46**, 79, 88
  Rennes 27
Chatterton, P. 4, 112, 116, 117
Chiasson vs NYC 1988 51–2
childcare services 93
Chile 8, 31, 62, 70–1
cleaners 87, 91, 92, 109
climate change 40, 57
closure of venues 6, 45, 52, 80, 89
  Fabric nightclub 45, 48–9
Colombia
  Cali 29, 72
  see also Bogota, Colombia
commissions, night-time 14, 15, 17, 35
  functions 36–7
  governing from within 25–8, 29, 30

London Night Time Commission 26, 45–6, **47**
San Francisco Entertainment Commission 14, 15, 17, 28
independent 14, 24, 31–5, 78
Berlin Club Commission 3, 6, 14, 15, 33, 68, 69
Zurich Bar and Club Commission 14, 15, 34–5
timeline *16*
consultancies 20, 69, 80, 90, 116
consultation on the night-time, collective 35–7, 54–5, 57
COVID-19 pandemic 24, 96–103
decentralizing of nightlife 101–2
disruptions to NTE 96–7, 101–3
focus on NTE recovery post 60, 67, 73
fragility of many businesses 100
impact on homelessness 97–8, 99
informal economy and 100–1
interrupting of nightlife 101–3
key workers 92, 94
night-time workers and 97, 98–100
Crary, J. 4, 57, 62, 113
creative spaces and communities 4, 6
in Berlin 67–8, 69
decentralizing 101–2
importance to London 44, 45, 50
managing Sydney's 28, 60
crime 12, 49, 79
restrictive policies to reduce 44, 55, 71–2, 102
'soft' deterrents 13–14, 15, 79
cultural policy in night-time planning 78
Czech Republic 17

D
dance venues 51–2, 66
definitions of 'night' 4–5
drinking programmes, responsible 72
Drozdzewski, D. 20, 114, 115
drugs 17, 44, 48–9
Dunn, N. 113–14, 117

E
Edensor, T. 7, 112, 113–14
Eldridge, A. 114, 115
entrepreneurialism, urban 20
Ernst & Young 90
Espinal, R. 27, 52
excluded and marginalized groups 44, 85–6, 86–7, 89–90, 108
addressing issue of 93–4

F
Fabric nightclub 45, 48–9
Fort Lauderdale, USA 25–6
France
night-workers' report 82

Paris 3, 13, 27, 92
Rennes 27, 36
Toulouse 34
see also Nantes, France

G
Geld, S., van der 32
Gelders, M. 7, 13, 14, 16, 19, 24, 115
gender issues after hours 2–3, 79, 87, 88, 108
Geneva, Switzerland 20, 33
gentrification 44, 53, 69, 89–90
Georgia 31
Germany *see* Berlin, Germany
global city 45, 54, 59, 68
Global Cities After Dark 37, 57
Global Night Time Recovery Plan 37, 40, 116
Gonzalez, J.C. 31, 71
governance *see* night-time governance of night-time economy (NTE)
Gwiazdzinski, L. 1, 114

H
Hackney, restrictions on opening hours in 46–8
Hadfield, P. 12, 44, 81, 88, 114, 115, 116
health
disparities 91
and night-time planning 40
of night-time workers in COVID-19 pandemic 97
risks of night-time working 82, 92, 99
sex workers 93, 99
healthcare workers 39, 74, 75, 82, 87, 90–1, 92, 93, 94
Hobbs, D. 4, 6, 116, 117
Hollands, R. 4, 112, 116, 117
homelessness 94, 97–8, 99
Hospitality Alliance 13, 51, 52, 77

I
inequalities, night-time 44, 85–6, 108–9
literature on 116–17
planning to address 93–4
informal economy 100–1
infrastructure 17
see also transport
injustice and urban night 86–90, 109
invisibilization 85, 90–3, 93–4
Iowa City, USA 29

J
Japan *see* Tokyo, Japan
Japan Nighttime Economy Association (JNEA) 64–5, 66, 67
Japan Tourism Agency 64, 67
Johnson, B. 26, 45, 82

K
Kelly, H. 114, 115

Khan, S. 26, 45, 48, 49
knowledge exchange grant 57
Kolvin, P. 45
Kyba, C. 7, 114

L
Lamé, A. 26, 45, 48, 79
Leichsenring, L. 69, 116
Les Pierrots de la Nuit 13
LGBTQI+ communities 44, 89, 108, 117
  closure of venues for 89
  night mayors representing 15–17
  Venues Charter **46**
licensee forums 58, 77
Licensing Act 2003 44
licensing policies 4, 5, 12, 115
  24 hour 67, 68–9, 73, 78, 102
  in Colombia 73
    'Carrot Law' (*Ley Zanahoria*) 71–2
    Safe Seal (*Sello Seguro*) 72–3
  contestation over restrictions in
    Hackney 46–8
  COVID -19 pandemic and New York's
    relaxing of 101
  discriminatory UK 44, 89
  in Sydney 54
  in Tokyo 66
Liempt, I., van 18, 86, 114, 115
literature review 111–17
  general introductions to night-time
    studies 113–14
  night-time inequalities 116–17
  night-time policy and non-governmental
    initiatives 115–16
  night-time politics and planning 114–15
Local 802 51–2
'lockout laws' 3, 55, 102
London First 57, 78
London, UK 26, 43–50, **46**, 86
  as a 24-hour city 44–6
  attempted closure of Fabric
    nightclub 45, 48–9
  charters, nightlife **46**, 79, 88
  corporate forms of nightlife 69
  discriminatory licensing policies 44, 89
  emergence of NTE as an object for
    policy 43–4
  'night czar' 6, 26, 45, 79, 84
  'night surgeries' 84
  Night Time Commission 26, 45–6, **47**
  night-time transport 2, 49–50, 88–9, 90
    Night Tube 2, 49, 81, 89
  NITE Night Spaces Conference 37
  NTE management resources 77
  opening hours in Hackney 46–8
  Think Night report 45–6, **47**
  urban safety and gender issues 2–3, **46**,
    79, 88

M
Maggioli, M. 114
Manchester, UK 30, 77, 89, 98
marginalized and excluded groups 44, 85–6,
    86–7, 89–90, 108
  addressing issue of 93–4
Marshall, L. 44, 89, 117
Mateo, J.N. 7, 114, 115
McArthur, J. 20, 81, 89, 90
mediation role of night-time offices 15, 17,
    23, 24–5, 79
Melbourne, Australia 53, 57, 58–61, 77, 80
  safe city strategies 79
Mexico 34
migrant workers 92, 94
Milan, M. 14–15, 29, 32, 116
Montreal, Canada 33–4
music venues 12
  in Berlin 67–8, 69
  closures and threat of closures 5–6, 45, 52
  Local 802 challenging legal discrimination
    against 51–2
  managing tensions over noise complaints 80
  in Melbourne 58–9
  proposed developments close to 6, 17,
    69, 80
Music Victoria 58

N
Nantes, France 26, 80, 81
  safety and gender issues 79
  sex workers 93
Netherlands 13–14, 14–15
  see also Amsterdam, Netherlands
networking night-time governance 18–21,
    37, 57, 58
New York Nightlife Association (NYNA)
    (formerly New York Cabaret
    Association (NYCA)) 51
New York Police Department (NYPD) 51,
    52, 77
New York, USA 27, 50–2
  'best practice' guide for nightlife venues 51,
    52, 77
  'Cabaret Law' 51, 52
  COVID-19 pandemic 98, 101
  growth in NTE 50
  Hospitality Alliance 13, 51, 52, 77
  Nightlife Advisory Board 27, 50–1, 52
  Office of Nightlife 27, 50–1, 52, 60
Nicholls, E. 7, 117
night buses 49, 50, 81, 90
night councils 14
  collective consultation on the
    night-time 35–6
  functions 36–7
  governing from within 25–8
  independent 31–5

night mayors 3, 14–18, 23, 106
  Amsterdam 3, 14–15, 32, 78
  attempt to appoint in Melbourne 60
  global distribution 17, *19*
  responsibilities 15–17
  timeline *16*
  urban entrepreneurialism and 20
night-time economy (NTE) 1–2, 12
  agendas 39–40, 77–9
  'core' and 'wider' 4, 39, 90
  COVID-19 pandemic and 60, 67, 94,
    96–7, 101–3
  emergence in urban policy discourse 43–4
  ethical issues 92, 109
  as a foundational economy 108
  informal economy 100–1
  injustices obscured in 44, 86–90, 108
  'missing' issues 40
  as a political issue 38
  reframing 'economy' in 85–6
  reproducing broader injustices 109
  resources and information targeted at 77
  see also night-time governance of night-time
    economy (NTE); night-time workers
night-time governance of night-time
    economy (NTE) 2–6
  actors in 11–14
  in Berlin 33, 62, 67–9
  in Bogota 62–3, 71–3
  and COVID-19 pandemic 24, 102–3
  expanding remit 23–4
  from inside local government 24, 25–31
  in London 26, 43–50, **46**
  in Melbourne 58–61
  movement towards 6–10
  networking 18–21, 37, 57, 58
  in New York 27, 50–2
  night councils and consultative
    mechanisms 35–7
  night mayors 14–18, *19*, 23
  from outside local government 24, 31–5
  pendulum effect between restrictive and
    enabling traditions of 102
  propositions 104–10
    enjoying city at night remains a
      privilege 108–9
    explicit role in urban governance 106–7
    need for a broader approach to
      planning 107
    need for night-time evidence 109–10
    NTE is a foundational economy 108
    NTEs reproducing broader injustices 109
    responsibility for sustainability 110
    varying night-time priorities 107–8
  in Sydney 28, 53–8
  in Tokyo 63–7
  in Valparaiso 31, 70–1
  variety of models but similar agendas 37–41

  where it should take place 23–5
night-time workers 90–3
  cleaners 87, 91, 92, 109
  COVID-19 pandemic shedding a light
    on 97, 98–100
  economic importance of 78
  gendered division of work 85
  health risks 82, 92, 99
  healthcare workers 39, 74, 75, 82, 87,
    90–1, 92, 93, 94
  improving working conditions 92–3,
    108, 109
  invisibility of paid and unpaid 85–6,
    90, 109
  migrant 92, 94
  navigating cities 87, 88, 89, 90, 92, 93,
    94, 108
  and online shopping 92, 94
  planning for 82–3, 108
  rights and fair pay 76
  sex workers 93, 99–100, 108
  shift work 82
  in Sydney 56
nightclubs and bars 12
  attempted closure of Fabric 45, 48–9
  relaxing of laws in Tokyo 64
  representing interests of 14, 15, 23, 30, 33,
    34–5, 68, 69, 77
  restricted opening hours in Hackney 46–8
  in Sydney 54, 55
  see also licensing policies
noise 17, 80
  actions to prevent, disturbances 13, 17,
    51, 80
non-governmental sector
  bottom-up governance in Berlin 68–9
  and collective consultation on night-
    time 35–7, 54–5, 57
  consultancies 20, 69, 80, 90, 116
  independent commissions, councils and
    offices 14, 15, 24, 31–5, 78, 84
  literature on night-time policy and
    initiatives from 115–16
  public partnerships with 5, 24–5, 51, 52,
    66–7, 71, 108
  trade organizations 13, 30, 51, 52, 57,
    77, 78
NTIA (Night Time Industries
    Association) 30
nurses 82, 87, 90, 91–2

O
online shopping 92, 94
'Open Sydney' 28, 54, 56, 57
Orlando, USA 17, 30, 80

P
Paloma 93
panels, advisory 28, 30, 36, 60–1

Paraguay 32–3, 72, 80
Paris, France 3, 13, 27, 92
'pendulum effect' in night-time
  governance 102
Pittsburgh, USA 30, 77
planning, night-time 75–6, 83–4
  'agent of change' principle and 58–9, 80
  cultural policy in 78
  individualized strategies needed for 107–8
  intersection between health and 40
  literature on politics and 114–15
  need for a broader approach to 107
  for night-time workers 82–3, 108
  towards inclusive 93–4
  transport and logistics 81–2, 87–90
planning, residential development 6, 17,
  69, 80
policing, night-time 12, 71–2, 87, 102
  collaborative partnerships 51, 52, 77
  discrimination in 87, 89, 94
'policy mobility' 18–20, 37, 57, 107
politics in night-time governance 38, 41
  in Bogota 71–3
  literature on planning and 114–15
  in New York 51–2
  in Sydney 53–8
  in Tokyo 64, 66–7
  in Valparaiso 70–1
'politics of difference' 88, 89, 93
Prague, Czech Republic 17
public–private partnerships 5, 24–5, 51, 52,
  66–7, 71, 108
public transport 17, 66, 81–2, 87, 93, 108
  in Berlin 69
  in London 2, 49–50, 81, 89, 90
  in Melbourne 58
  night buses 49, 50, 81, 90
  night-time workers' navigation of 87, 88,
    89, 90, 92, 93, 94, 108
  safety fears over use of 49, 87, 88
  see also transport
pubs 47, 77

R
racial exclusion in NTE 44, 89, 108
Rennes, France 27, 36
residential development planning 6, 17,
  69, 80
residents, local 80
  attempted closure of Fabric nightclub 48–9
  controversy over opening hours in
    Hackney 46–8
Resilient Cities Initiative 57
'Responsible Partying' (Farra en la Buena) 73
ride-hailing services 17, 49, 50, 72, 88
right to the city 34, 40, 59, 117
Roberts, M. 4, 5, 6, 12, 80, 86, 114, 115
Robin, E. 18, 43, 83, 86, 92, 95

Robinson, J. 2, 43, 106
Rotterdam, Netherlands 13, 14
Rough Nights 82
'route angels' 72

S
Safe Seal (Sello Seguro) 72–3
safety, urban 2–3, 79, 87
  Citizen Safety Division, Valparaiso 31, 71
  'Responsible Partying'in Bogota 73
  travel and 49, 87, 88
  Women's Night Safety Charter 46, 79, 88
San Francisco, USA 28
  Entertainment Commission 14, 15, 17, 28
  noise assessments and planning
    reviews 17, 80
  NTE management resources 77
San Luis Potosi, Mexico 34
scales of night-time governance 38
  in Berlin 67–9
  in Sydney 55–6, 57
  in Tokyo 63–7
scientific research on night-time 112, 114
Seijas, A. 5, 7, 13, 14, 15, 17, 24, 31, 71, 73,
  95, 102, 115, 116
sex workers 93, 99–100, 108
sexual violence 87, 88
Sharp, J. 31, 70, 71
Shaw, R. 6, 7, 20, 41, 44, 90, 113, 117
Sheller, M. 87–8
shelters 94, 98
Shibuya, Japan 65, 66
Smeds, E. 49, 81, 82, 85, 86, 88
social reproduction 85, 86–7, 108
Sound Diplomacy 5, 17, 20, 73, 80, 116
'square hosts' 14, 15, 79
Stichting N8BM A'DAM 15
Straw, W. 2, 7, 23, 41, 114, 115
surveillance equipment 12
sustainability 92, 110
Sweden 93
Switzerland
  Geneva 20, 33
  Zurich 14, 15, 34–5
Sydney, Australia 20, 28, 53–8
  citizen and business consultations 54–5
  a clash of scales 55–6
  Committee for Sydney 57
  corporate forms of nightlife 69
  Global Cities After Dark forums 37, 57
  Greater Sydney 24-hour Economy Strategy 56
  history of regulation 53–5
  institutionalizing the 24-hour city 56–8
  knowledge exchange grant 57
  Late Night Trading Development Control
    Plan 54
  Liquor Act 2007 54
  'lockout laws' 3, 55, 102

Night Time Economy Commission 57
Nightlife and Creative Sector Advisory
    Panel 28, 60–1
'Open Sydney' 28, 54, 56, 57
size of NTE 53, 55
Sydney as a 24-hour City 57

T

Talbot, D. 7, 44, 81, 86, 88, 89, 90, 116, 117
taxi services 17, 49, 50, 72, 88
Tbilisi, Georgia 31
temporal boundaries of 'night' 4–5
Think Night report 45–6, **47**
Tokyo, Japan 62, 63–7
    24-Hour Tokyo Promotion
        Committee 66–7
    local level, ward-driven innovations 64–5,
        66
    metropolitan level management 66, 67
    Night Time Economy Association 66
    nightlife history 63–4
    Shibuya 65, 66
    tourism 64, 65, 66, 67
Toronto, Canada 98
Toulouse, France 34
tourism
    in Berlin 68
    cultural policy and 78
    in Tokyo 64, 65, 66, 67
    in Valparaiso 70, 71
trade organizations 13, 30, 51, 52, 57, 77, 78
transport
    in Bogota 72
    focus on consumers rather than workers 89
    infrastructure 17
    justice 87–8
    planning for 81–2, 87–90
    'route angels' 72
    taxi services 17, 49, 50, 72, 88
    in Tokyo 65, 66
    see also public transport
Transport for London (TfL) 49, 50, 90
twenty-four hour cities 4
    Amsterdam 78, 102
    Berlin 67, 68–9
    Bogota 73
    London 44–6
    Melbourne 58, 60

Sydney 56–8
Tokyo 66–7

U

Uber 17, 72
    in London 49, 50, 88
    underground night scene 12, 51, 72
United Kingdom (UK)
    Aberdeen 29, 36
    Manchester 30, 77, 89, 98
    see also London, UK
United States of America (USA)
    Fort Lauderdale 25–6
    Iowa City 29
    Orlando 17, 30, 80
    Pittsburgh 30, 77
    Washington DC 17
    see also New York, USA; San
        Francisco, USA
Urban Studies 115

V

Valparaiso, Chile 8, 31, 62, 70–1
Vergès, F. 85, 87, 90–1
Vibe Lab 20, 116
vision documents 75–6
volunteers 13–14, 15, 52, 79
vulnerable groups 79, 87–8, 94, 107
    and COVID-19 pandemic 98–101

W

Washington DC, USA 17
We Love Hackney (WLH) 47–8
Wolifson, P. 20, 57, 114, 115
women
    cleaners 91
    homeless 94
    safety at night 2–3, 49, 79, 87, 88
    social reproduction work 85, 86–7
Women's Night Safety Charter **46**, 79, 88

Y

Yarra, city of, Australia 53, 58, 59
Young Foundation 82, 83

Z

Zeebra 66
zoning 12, 51, 79, 101
Zurich, Switzerland 14, 15, 34–5

www.ingramcontent.com/pod-product-compliance
Lightning Source LLC
Chambersburg PA
CBHW062109040426
42336CB00042B/2702